Praise for Arthur Samuel Joseph

"As with any renowned brand—personal or professional—projecting who you are with authenticity and in one voice is paramount to success. The Vocal Awareness Method to Communication Mastery is a powerful tool that will ensure your voice as a leader, innovator, or captain of industry is resounding."

—Herve Humler, president and COO
of The Ritz-Carlton Hotel Company

"Gifted master Arthur Joseph has a gift of voice and almost 50 years of sharing and teaching his extraordinary gift. There are numerous books on what to say and how to speak, but only a truly gifted teacher can teach us how to connect to others through the extra dimension of our voice."

—Daniel Yun, CEO of Belstar Group

"Whether you are an executive looking to influence the board, a leader looking to inspire your team, or a speaker looking to engage a crowd, at the core is realizing the personal power of your voice. Arthur Joseph's focus on the mastery of specific rituals and the development of one's persona enables individuals to unleash their unique inner strength and achieve empowerment through voice!"

—Cherita McIntye, PhD,
director of executive learning at ESPN

"Arthur Joseph is without peer in developing communication and presentation skills. His use of technique, coupled with passion and belief, combine for a spiritual approach to mastering communication skills—to present who you truly are and what you represent as a form of self-fulfillment."

—John Branca, entertainment attorney
and coexecutor of the Michael Jackson Estate

"What I love most about Arthur is that his guidance is about so much more than just work, it is about life. It is about being the greatest YOU possible and bringing out the natural YOU in a meaningful, authentic way. Arthur speaks of the need for repetition, creating good habits in any form of communication, and enjoying the process of practice, practice, practice!"

—Julie Foudy, ESPN/ABC analyst and reporter, two-time World Cup champion, two-time Olympic gold medalist, and former captain of the U.S. Women's Soccer Team

"The guidance of Arthur Joseph allowed me to accelerate my trajectory in the competitive world of broadcast journalism. Arthur gave me the necessary tools to continue to improve my voice and on-air presence to this day. It was one of the greatest investments in my career."

—Andrea Canning, *Dateline NBC* correspondent

"As the daughter of a Tuskegee Airman, striving for perfection was at the epicenter of my existence—a paradigm that paralyzed me, despite my incredible giftedness. Even as a masterful presenter, I spoke with a throttle in my throat—from a place of pleasing others, rather than honoring myself. That shifted when Arthur Joseph, my own personal Yoda, entered my life. Practicing 7 rituals for 7 minutes 7 days a week allowed me to surrender to my truth and step in stature into my power. Vocal Awareness released me to joyfully claim my Voice—and my greatness. *Vocal Leadership* will positively impact the trajectory of your professional and personal life forever!"

—Anne Palmer, Emmy Award–winning talk show host and author of *The Gifted Trap*

"When I entered the world of broadcasting, because of my media history, I thought it would be an easy transition. I quickly realized that performing in broadcasting goes well beyond just knowing what you are talking about. It also requires listening, presence, pace, breathing, and so much more. I found myself simply treading water to stay afloat, but not making progress. Enter Arthur Joseph, and all of that changed. Arthur taught me the little things that I had never even considered. He taught me the art of breathing and showed me how it is the lifeline for a broadcaster, when I thought we all knew how to do it! He taught me how to enhance my personality so that it shows up at a performance level while never compromising the essence of what makes me unique. I could go on and on about the impact that Arthur has had on my new career, but I think the best way to describe his impact is by using an old adage that I carried with me while competing in the NFL, 'The difference between good and great is in the details.' Arthur has taught me what those details are and how to attack each one of them so that I have a chance to pursue greatness in my new career (broadcasting/speaking) just as I did in my old one!"

—Kurt Warner, Super Bowl XXXIV–winning quarterback
of the St. Louis Rams and NFL Network analyst

"Arthur Joseph took rookie reporters in their first jobs out of school and turned them into network news correspondents within a few years. Even if you have no plans of becoming the next Walter Cronkite or Katie Couric, you need this book. Learning how to communicate more effectively will give you a huge advantage, both at work and in life."

—Jim Morris, former executive producer at Channel One News

"I grew up with a stutter and struggled with it my entire life, so it seemed a mismatch for me to become a broadcaster. But as I've studied Vocal Awareness, the knowledge, dedication, and compassion Arthur has shown me has allowed me to conquer my fear of public speaking. It has made a dramatic difference in my personal life as well. More than that, Arthur has helped me see the Champion that lives within and identify how a Champion lives, thinks, breathes—and apply this understanding to my broadcasting. I encourage everyone to learn from Arthur Samuel Joseph, the master of the voice, and find the Champion within."

—Jeff Emig, Supercross/Motocross Champion, member of the Motorcycle Hall of Fame, and television broadcaster

"Arthur Samuel Joseph is not only a master of communication, he also has the ability to turn those who follow his guidance into masters themselves. Please do not just listen to what Arthur tells you to do, rather put it in action. His guidance will change the quality of your voice, your communication, and the power of your delivery."

—Dov Baron, founder of Full Monty Leadership

"As a collegiate and professional football coach for 28 years, I have had few regrets. One is never winning a Super Bowl, but coming very close. Another is not having met Arthur Joseph *during* my coaching career. Coaching is teaching, and teaching is communicating. There is no doubt in my mind that I would have been a better communicator with my players, staff, and the media had I applied what I've learned from Arthur's Vocal Awareness Method. I know it will be interesting and beneficial to you as well."

—Steve Mariucci, former head coach of the San Francisco 49ers and the Detroit Lions and NFL Network analyst

"Arthur's results with his clients are subtle at times, but always meaningful. His passion for his work is immense. He brings out the best in people with his unique ability to connect with them—even spiritually at times. He empowers his clients to become better people and it is reflected in their actions."

—Eric Weinberger, executive producer at NFL Network

"Arthur is the true master of communication, in business and in life. He has proven to be the go-to expert on how to use our vocal skills to be better people, better professionals—the best we can be!"

—Doug Harward, founder and CEO of TrainingIndustry.com

"Arthur has demonstrated time and time again a special skill of decisively communicating to many high-profile athletes and broadcasters the most effective use of one's own voice. His dedication to his well-developed philosophies on the proper use of speech is admired greatly."

—Dick Maxwell, former NFL senior director of broadcasting

"Arthur Joseph is a brilliant and insightful teacher who exhibits mastery in everything he does. He taught me many things, including that a deeper more resonant voice is more trustworthy. His principles are essential for powerful and effective communication."

—Marcia Wieder, founder and CEO of Dream University

"I cannot recommend Vocal Awareness enough. Arthur's method has been integral in helping me overcome my nervousness when speaking in front of groups, as well as giving me confidence for live television spots. Speaking clearly and with awareness is the one technique I recommend to all my franchisees, and it has helped me in countless ways both professionally and personally. The success of his method allows you to accentuate your true self, a better self. The end result is the unique position of becoming more assertive and powerful, while at the same time speaking with compassion and thoughtfulness."

—Jaime Van Wye, founder and CEO of Zoom Room, Inc.

"Arthur led me on the peaceful path to Vocal Awareness at a critical time in my career. His practical yet profound voice work changed the course of my professional destiny. He helped me to uncover my greatest gifts and talents and to channel them in service and contribution to others."

—Deborah Torres Patel, CEO of Expressing You!®

"Arthur is a master at teaching us to vocally embody our most powerful, authentic, and loving Self. If you are ready to do this, read this book!"

—Steve Farrell, worldwide coordinating director
at Humanity's Team

"Working with Arthur changed my life! Not only did my voice and stamina change dramatically, but my true voice emerged. I felt more comfortable, authentic, and confident in my work. Many shifts occurred on several different levels. I recommend Arthur to everyone. Working with him is powerful and produces results."

—Karen Dietz, PhD, owner of Polaris Associates
Consulting, Inc., and Just Story It

"The Vocal Awareness Method has led to a happier and more authentic life, as well as an exceptional and sustainable impact on my business. I am a leader, manager, trainer, performer, and the founder and director of a global music and rhythm consultancy business serving business schools, NGOs, and some of the world's leading companies. What Arthur has taught me influences how I deal and resonate with my teams, clients, and the audiences that I work and play with. Arthur is unfailingly dedicated to making a difference, and he teaches communication mastery with sincere concern and deep love."

—Doug Manuel, founder and director
of Sewa Beats International, Switzerland

"Vocal Awareness has been the very essence of my transcendence from good to great. After years of teaching others as a communication trainer, the pathway to excellence has been in my discovery of the inner spirit of Voice through Arthur Samuel Joseph. This work is for masters. Do not delay your metamorphosis from ordinary to extraordinary."

—Ricky (The Voice) Lien,
CEO of Mindset Media Pte Ltd, Singapore

"Some days I ask myself, 'How is it that you are able to express your voice with such ease?' I immediately go to a place of abundant gratitude knowing that a wise, creative, masterful being by the name of Arthur Joseph inspired and instilled Vocal Awareness within me at a vital point on my path. As I continue blossoming into my soul's highest expression, I'm humbled and joyous to know that I will embody and emanate the calling—to be, to create, to collaborate—through the vessel of this voice."

—Ellie Drake, founder of BraveHeartWomen.com

"Vocal Awareness isn't a parlor trick Vocal Awareness begins with me. Arthur first helped me to recognize and accept the power I had within. Then I had to embrace the person I wanted to be. My voice became my instrument that showed that person to the world. The difficulty was staying in touch with that persona not just during a presentation, but in hospital corridors, at my son's basketball game, or in a restaurant. As I became more aware, I was astounded by the change in power in my voice. I could hear it on the video; I could see it on the tape. Others noticed it on my voice mail message. I was truly heard in meetings and looked to for input. Mastery takes years, and I still have miles to go, but I am on the path and I embrace the journey. I am forever indebted to Vocal Awareness. Now, I don't have to play the role of the confident, empathic surgeon, that is who I am."

—Melanie B. Kinchen, MD, orthopedic spine surgeon

"Vocal Awareness isn't as much about smart communication as it is about helping you discover the YOU that you never knew existed. Arthur's method has inspired me to celebrate and embody the uniqueness that only I bring to the world. It's that level of authenticity which I've discovered distinguishes the greatest of communicators."

—Moe Abdou, founder and principal of 33voices.com

"Working with Arthur was an essential piece establishing and growing my brand and perfecting my craft. Beyond business, the lessons I continue to learn with Arthur ground me, make me a better person, and allow me to have great confidence and certainty in reaching my goals and dreams. No matter what you do, understanding how you communicate and connect with people through Vocal Awareness is an essential part of owning your power."

—Shira Lazar, host and executive producer of *What's Trending*

"Arthur's persistence, care, and wisdom allowed me to discover my Voice, a liberating life-changing experience. The course he delivered within a cross-functional setting of a corporate team with some key business partners brought deep learning and remarkable team performance. Innovation, organizational agility, competitiveness, and value creation occur when people communicate in Vocal Awareness at the intersections of their experience and expertise."

—Robert de Liefde, global tax expert,
Geneva, Switzerland

"Understanding and practicing the art of communication is critical to success in business and in life. Arthur's innate ability to listen and teach this art affords him the unique ability to truly transform our approach to what we say, how we say it, and the way in which our words will be received."

—Laurie Orlando, senior vice president of talent planning
and development at ESPN

VOCAL
LEADERSHIP

7 Minutes a Day to Communication Mastery

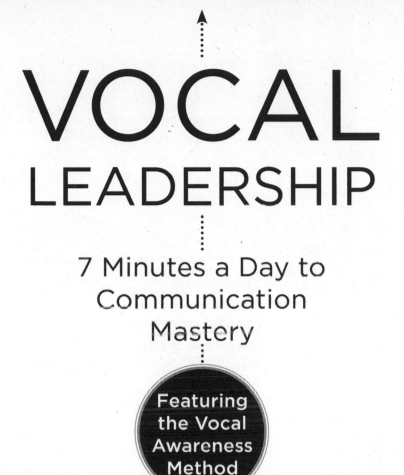

Featuring the Vocal Awareness Method

ARTHUR SAMUEL JOSEPH

New York Chicago San Francisco Athens London Madrid Mexico City
Milan New Delhi Singapore Sydney Toronto

1 2 3 4 5 6 7 8 9 0   DOC/DOC   1 9 8 7 6 5 4 3

ISBN 978-0-07-180771-5
MHID 0-07-180771-3

e-ISBN 988-0-07-180772-2
e-MHID 0-07-180772-1

Library of Congress Cataloging-in-Publication Data

Joseph, Arthur.
  Vocal leadership : 7 minutes a day to communication mastery / by Arthur Samuel Joseph.
      pages cm
  ISBN 978-0-07-180771-5 (hardback) — ISBN 0-07-180771-3
  1. Voice culture. I. Title.
  PN4162.J665 2013
  302.2'242—dc23   2013017768

McGraw-Hill Education books are available at special quantity discounts to use as premiums and sales promotions or for use in corporate training programs. To contact a representative, please visit the Contact Us pages at www.mhprofessional.com.

*To three generations of students and clients
for their dedicated commitment to the Work*

CONTENTS

FOREWORD

The late Steve Sabol once said something about Vince Lombardi, the legendary Hall of Fame coach of the Green Bay Packers, that always stuck with me.

Steve was the creative genius behind NFL Films. To be a great filmmaker like Steve, you had to be an expert communicator. One day in his office, where Steve kept a framed, autographed photo of Lombardi on the wall, we started talking about what made Coach Lombardi so special. Steve made a very interesting observation about Lombardi that I had never heard before.

"Lombardi had this great voice," Steve said. "He sounded like a general out of central casting. He made you listen."

Steve's point was that Lombardi's voice—and the way he used it—was an important element of his success as a leader.

Steve's story about Coach Lombardi came to mind when I learned a few years ago about the work that Arthur Joseph was doing with some of our NFL Network talent. They raved about Arthur's Vocal Awareness Method, which teaches you how to use your entire body, especially your voice, to more effectively convey your message. He helped them become better communicators in any setting, from reporting and analyzing on NFL Network to delivering Hall of Fame acceptance speeches to presenting a business plan to potential investors.

Since communication is such an important part of leadership in any area of business, we decided to introduce Arthur's method to others in the NFL. He has worked successfully with numerous executives in our office, including me. We have learned that elevating your game as a verbal communicator takes much more than putting words on a page and reading and memorizing them.

How you convey the right words through the use of your voice and other physical elements—your eyes, your facial expressions, your hands, your body stature—can make a big difference between success and failure as a communicator. Arthur Joseph's Vocal Awareness Method forces you to define yourself so that you can express yourself naturally. It is a very personal journey.

Like any other challenge, learning Arthur's method and becoming a stronger communicator takes time and hard work. It is a process. It takes practice. There are specific techniques that will make a powerful impact on your ability to be a better leader.

For anyone aspiring to improve as a leader, no matter your line of work, I highly recommend taking the time to learn more about Arthur Joseph's Vocal Awareness Method for true leadership. Don't underestimate the importance of your voice and its enormous potential for making a positive difference in your personal life, your business life, and the organization you represent.

Roger Goodell
Commissioner of the National Football League

ACKNOWLEDGMENTS

I would be remiss if I did not begin this brief acknowledgment by thanking my family—Rebecca, Isaac, and Eli. You each inspire me daily to be the best I can possibly be. Vocal Awareness is my Work, but you are my life.

As I have said in past books, none of the work that I am privileged to do would have manifested without the love, sacrifice, dedication, and steadfast belief of my late mother, Betty. She was the first to help me know that dreams could come true.

Casey Ebro, my editor at McGraw-Hill Education, thank you for seeing the *Wall Street Journal* article on Vocal Awareness and sending the initial e-mail. Your trust, friendship, and commitment to excellence were reflected from our first conversation through the final edits of this book.

Deep appreciation also to Mary Glenn, associate publisher at McGraw-Hill Education. Taking time away to step out of your meeting on my first visit to your offices, sitting down, and truly engaging spoke volumes.

To Jane Palmieri, editing manager, and Cheryl Hudson, senior production supervisor, at McGraw-Hill Education, for your patience and creative guidance.

To Gail Ross, my agent at the Ross-Yoon Agency, for your belief in me and in my vision.

To the Team Leader for almost 30 years, Stacey Beth Torchon. You embody Spiritual Pragmatism, and as I've said throughout this book, "the same person shows up everywhere."

My Education Chair, Elizabeth Harmetz. You came into the studio many years ago as an extraordinary singer/teacher and trusted that I could help you fulfill your vision to become even more. Thank you for your devotion and contribution.

Jeanne James, you have sustained an earnestness to Vocal Awareness for many years. Your patience and insight in helping me birth this book are exemplary.

To the Commissioner of the National Football League, Roger Goodell, who truly does what it takes to "represent the Shield," thank you for writing the foreword.

I am grateful to so many who have taken the time to write testimonials from across the United States and around the world.

To the students, clients, institutions, businesses, and broadcast networks around the globe who have allowed me to teach—thank you.

I am so privileged and humbled to do the Work and have the opportunities life presents. I am in awe. Each day in my spiritual focus when in prayer and meditation, I acknowledge Source and strive to be in service.

INTRODUCTION

The Vocal Awareness Method to Achieve Communication Mastery

*The only person you are destined to become
is the person you decide to be.*

—Ralph Waldo Emerson

This book is the culmination of almost five decades of teaching Vocal Awareness. One underlying theme is, *Voice Is Power.* When we own our Voice, we own our power. To own the power of our Voice is not merely to be loud or vocally or verbally aggressive, rather through our Voice and our communication, to authentically *be* who we are, literally—in *every* communication, to embody in a consciously aware way the *message* and the *messenger*.

For years, you have desired to confidently communicate both the message and the messenger comfortably and emboweringly, authentically and easily at all times but, until you opened this book, you were never shown how—to not only *own* your vocal power but to *own your power*—not merely intellectually, philosophically, or in a professional context because you have business acumen, but cohesively and consistently at all times.

In business, the premise is, no matter what our educational background, career path or position, the implicit understanding in the way we speak is who we are. That may seem reasonable. However, it is a foundation built on quicksand. Whether it is a job interview, a board meeting, media event, teleconference, PowerPoint presentation, strategic planning meeting, or delivering a keynote address—the reality is we don't know there is a better way to deliver our message, thus we settle for the way we have always done it because *speaking is habit*. The way we sit, stand, walk, talk, breathe, and look at one another speaks volumes.

In the arts or athletics, one is taught how to do something and how and why not to do something. Consistent practice over many years helps achieve mastery. But in everyday conversation/business discourse, one is not taught basic fundamentals: breathing techniques; vocal warm-ups; effective body language; vocal projection (without raising pitch); appropriate tempo; verbal/nonverbal expression; persona/brand/clarity about identity—how do we want to be known?

There is a better way to Communication Mastery: *Vocal Leadership*. This concept is based on the trademarked Vocal Awareness Method: Empowerment through Voice. A method built not on quicksand but on a solid foundation of firm principles and proven techniques. It has been taught for decades to thousands of people from all walks of life throughout the United States and around the globe.

In Vocal Awareness, first we discover that we thought we knew how to communicate effectively. Then we discover that we do not know this. Finally, we discover that we have a choice in how we communicate and that *we are not our behaviors*.

Vocal Awareness is a new form of mastery. It is *Mastery through Communication*. It is a paradigm shift. Etymologically, the word *paradigm* has at its root the words *show* and *teaching*. This book provides successful learning strategies and proven techniques, *showing you* and *teaching you* how to speak, communicate, and embody the leader you are capable of being.

Through the practice of Vocal Awareness, Communication Mastery is possible. The root of the word *communication* derives from Latin which, in part, originally meant *to share*. It also meant to *join/unite/participate in*. The word *mastery* from *master* is the Latin word for *chief*. It is a source of the word *to magnify* or *magnitude*. In other words, the basic thesis of Communication Mastery is to magnify and share who we are in every communication—at all times. *The same person shows up everywhere*, and we *always* have a choice.

I am reminded of a client's remarks at the end of a recent Skype session, "It is so difficult to stay conscious all the time, but I recognize that is the '10,000 hours' and mastery is my goal." In these pages you will learn how to develop your vocal quality and maximize every moment. If you do not like your voice, you will learn to appreciate it and even, possibly, enjoy it. You will learn how to deliver every message consistently, intrapersonally and interpersonally, whether you are speaking with your peers, your subordinates, or your boss.

When learning something new, there is a tendency to be intimidated and/or overwhelmed by the information and the effort required. Often, we also subliminally do not believe that we can be successful. We tend to judge and doubt ourselves and our capacity for success. Nowhere does this sense of personal judgment more dramatically come into play than when we strive to discover our own voice and our consummate leadership ability. In this context please think of judgment as the dictionary definition implies, "the ability to make considered decisions or come to sensible conclusions."[1] Be discerning, not judgmental.

Be assured that the Vocal Awareness process will be unveiled systematically, step by step. Each technique and principle will be explained thoroughly and will build incrementally, chapter by chapter. There will be ample opportunity to apply the work in your daily life, personally and professionally. Throughout this book in myriad biographical stories, metaphors, how-to examples, and Action Steps closing each chapter, your skills and confidence will develop integratively. You will discover how to achieve mastery through communication. However, it is one thing to intellectually understand this; it is another to empirically embody it. Every element you need to know to authentically and confidently communicate and lead, as masterfully as possible, will be amplified and meticulously developed throughout the book. As the chapters unfold, you will acquire the skills necessary to implement and sustain not just Communication Mastery but yourself, as consciously commanding as possible. How do you want to be known as a leader?

Communication Mastery requires audacity. It is all about us—and yet has nothing to do with us. We are both the chalice that contains all that is possible and the vessel through which everything passes. We are responsible to ourselves and to the work we are called to do.

To be the best of our selves is our right, our opportunity, our responsibility.

Enjoy the journey to Communication Mastery.

1

COMMUNICATION MASTERY: THE JOURNEY BEGINS

The tones of human voices are mightier than
strings and brass to move the soul...
—Friedrich Klopstock

Voice Is Power—When I Own My Voice, I Own My Power

Voice has changed the world from the beginning of time. Imagine what the Prophet Abraham must have sounded like to compel others to follow him across the desert. In the last century BC, it was understood that comprehensive training was necessary to develop great communicators. There was a Roman system of oratory that taught public speakers about ideas, lines of argument, structure, organization, diction, style, physical delivery, and memory. Speeches could last for up to four hours and, as they were always spoken, never read, they were memorized. Quoting directly from the journal of the greatest Roman orator of the time, Marcus Tullius Cicero:

A leading speaker will vary and modulate his voice, raising and lowering it and deploying the full scale of tones. He will avoid extravagant gestures and stand impressively erect. He will not pace about and, when he does so, not for any distance. He should not dart forward, except in moderation with strict control. There should be no effeminate bending of the neck or twiddling of his fingers or beating out the rhythm of his cadences on his knuckles. He should control himself by the way he holds and moves his entire body. He should extend his arm at moments of high dispute, and lower it during calmer passages. Once he has made sure he does not have a stupid expression on his face and/or a grimace, he should control his eyes with great care for, as the face is the image of the soul, the eyes are its translators.

Moving forward in time, imagine hearing the actual tonal quality of Jesus delivering the Sermon on the Mount, Mohammad's sixth-century speeches that led to a movement and the creation of a new religion, or the voice of the Buddha communicating his truths.

Leap ahead to the twentieth century: The most reprehensible example of vocal power was Adolf Hitler. His voice, delivery, body language, and presence were diabolically aligned in such a way that they virtually usurped a people's will. At the same time, Franklin Delano Roosevelt and Winston Churchill successfully kept the free world together through the power of their voices via radio and public addresses. There was the gentle but commanding voice of Mahatma Gandhi helping unite his nation. In the second half of the twentieth century, other voices and their impactful communication style reverberate: In November 1954 on the television show *See It Now*, Edward R. Murrow confronted Senator Joseph McCarthy in an interview that changed the political course of America. In 1963, Walter Cronkite's tearful statement to the world reported the assassination of President John F. Kennedy. On August 28, 1963, the Reverend Martin Luther King Jr. stood before tens of thousands who listened to him proclaim "I Have a Dream" from the steps of the Lincoln Memorial.

Fidel Castro, Mao Tse Tung, Vaclav Havel, Nelson Mandela, Maya Angelou, Gloria Steinem, Bill and Hillary Clinton, and Aung San Suu Kyi are a handful of leaders who personify and integrate in their very essence the character of the individual, for right or wrong, for good or evil.

A handful of business leaders that come to mind include Warren Buffett, Bill Gates, Jack Welch, Steve Jobs, Mark Zuckerberg, Meg Whitman, Marissa Mayer, and Sheryl Sandberg whose drive, passion, belief system, and commitment are not simply communicated in their rhetoric, but embodied in the tones of their voices, through their body language, in the very sinews of who they are. It may seem intangible but, frankly, it is not. The examples I have illustrated run the gamut. There are clearly profound leaders worth emulating, but I would be remiss if I did not also identify despotic world leaders who have won over the masses through their communication styles, as well as successful business leaders who, albeit, successful corporate executives, may be abusive communicators in the office. Voice is power; it does not discriminate. It is how we wield this power that makes the difference. There is a vibrational quality, an energetic essence that can force a listener to follow the speaker's lead no matter what. This phenomenon is not illusory but foundational. In its most primal essence, *communication is vibration.* This communication is subliminally conveyed through pitch, timbre, volume, energy, willpower, conviction—these are but a few of the elements that compel us to listen. Whose voices today, whether they be an acclaimed world leader, a despot, a business leader, a social or community activist, or a media icon, will resonate through time—and are we even listening?

When Alexander Graham Bell invented the telephone in 1876, we began losing the art of letter writing. With the advent of high-speed technology, we have now begun to lose the art of public discourse. In the twenty-first century, we are in the age of what I call "fingers and thumbs." The Internet is our preferred mode of communication. We may actually spend more time typing our words than speaking them. Beyond this, the Internet creates anonymity. We do not have to physically engage or confront one another. We don't have to physically show up, be in the room in front of people—nobody sees or hears our voices—they only see our words. Most of us have probably been in situations at a gathering or at work where people in the same room are e-mailing, texting, and instant messaging one another rather than going over, making eye contact, and speaking. Because we tend to type fast, we also speak quickly with one another when we converse. When we type, we tend to convey data in sound bites rather than tell a story and communicate with complete and more complex thoughts. This mode of communication permeates our daily interactions whether trivial or, far more important, when we need to be tactical and deliver impactful messages. Subliminally or consciously, we are less comfortable doing so.

In the world of Internet communication, misspellings, typos, and poor punctuation are acceptable and have become the norm. How many e-mails and texts that we send or receive daily have errors in them? By extension, those typos become *verbal typos* in our conversation—what I call w*hite noise* such as "ums" and "uhs." This "normal" communication is not strategic. We are definitely not conscious or aware—we just speak. We have become inured in daily conversation and settle for being average. But *perception is reality*. When we are speaking, we are also personally being evaluated—subliminally or intentionally. In our personal lives, this is one thing; in politics, simplistic conversation—appearing average—becomes far more significant and the consequences potentially monumental.

We no longer expect leaders to be inspiring. There's a tendency to want them to speak more like us, where malapropisms and syntactical errors are acceptable.

In addition, in studies attributed to Albert Mehrabian, professor emeritus of psychology at the University of California, Los Angeles, beginning in the 1970s a theory was extrapolated as either the 7-38-55 Rule or the 8-37-55 Rule—that in all verbal communication, only 7 or 8 percent may be language-based or derived from the words themselves. This means that perhaps only 7 or 8 percent of everything we say is retained by our listener's unconscious mind.

An opinion is created in *three seconds*. Do you have difficulty verbally conveying an idea at all, let alone succinctly and strategically in every business situation from a job interview to a keynote speech, from answering the telephone to leading a board meeting? Whether it's running out of breath or gasping for air; feeling self-conscious; speaking too rapidly or with inordinate tongue/jaw or neck and shoulder tension; fidgeting with your fingers; sitting in a meeting jiggling your leg up and down; bustling down a hallway; speaking too high or too breathy; stammering; filling space with "ums" and "uhs" for fear that if you take a moment, you will be interrupted—these are only a few examples of how in everyday conversation we may reveal aspects of ourselves that we do not want anyone to see or know about.

When I speak at business schools, one of the first things I say is, "In the business world, people do not say to an individual, 'Your voice is tense or your voice is anxious.'" They may, however, say, "You are tense or you are anxious," or, frankly and more likely, not say anything at all. Rather, they will draw their own conclusions—right or wrong. How much would they retain from your presentation?

In a March 2012 *Wall Street Journal* interview, one of the tips I offered was that a meeting begins before you walk into the room and how you walk into the room matters. Do you convey confidence by, among other things, your physical presence and your nonverbal communication? In communication, it is not simply what we say but how we say it.

Almost a century ago, the American poet Robert Frost wrote: "Two roads diverged in a yellow wood . . ." From a communication perspective, global society is in those woods right now—which fork in the road will we take? The one that takes us down the path of mediocrity, ultimately dissolving into fractious societies where the loudest voice, even if it is that of a demagogue, is the norm— where people only carp, shout at one another, do not listen or hear. Or, do we take the other fork in the road, the one less traveled by—the one that requires us to communicate with one another honorably, commandingly, authentically, respectfully—listening to our own intrinsic inner voice and deliberately integrating it into our spoken voice. There is a choice to be made. The time is now. If we do not make it, we abdicate our responsibility to ourselves and thus to our future.

The path I am clearly advocating is Communication Mastery. As we continue the journey, just like standing at the fork in the yellow wood, it is a choice. We ultimately take responsibility. We learn how to communicate, claim our consummate vocal identity, and consistently allow the same person to show up everywhere.

Voice Is Power—Creating Our Own History

Voice Is Power. This statement has been expressed for millennia. And, as in most things to do with voice or communication, we believe we have a clear understanding of what this means. One interpretation implies vocal strength, as in, he or she has a loud voice. Another may imply vocal stamina, "Christine can speak for hours at our corporate events, and her voice never seems to tire." Or, "Jerry conveys strong leadership authority."

However, when speaking about voice or communication, what else is implied in the statement, "Voice is power"—character traits, for example? "Hector always seems so honest when he speaks with our customers." "Louise is a great sales associate. She is our most successful telemarketer. Our client surveys always reflect how trustworthy she seems over the phone when speaking." What other positive attributes come to mind? Caring, thoughtful, earnest, respectful, secure, authentic, friendly, happy, and so forth.

Or, the antithesis might be the case. "Charlotte is very aggressive with subordinates. Her staff doesn't feel she respects them and, because of this, productivity in her division is negatively impacted." "At the office, Richard appears so arrogant that colleagues are having trouble collaborating with him." Yet, a different type of example, "John seems so anxious when he speaks with everyone—his peers or his bosses. He is bright, but his seeming lack of confidence holds him back." Other negative attributes: insensitive, immature, disengaged, territorial, not trustworthy, self-serving, inauthentic, and so forth.

Voice is power. Vocal Awareness interprets this statement from a very specific perspective. First, literally—it means what it says. But, second, from a far more complex, comprehensive, depthful, insightful, yet clear and concise understanding, this interpretation understands that Voice reflects all of who we are intrapersonally—our inner Voice—our dreams, aspirations, fears, doubts, our very spiritual/ emotional/intellectual essence. The inner Voice is what is known in Vocal Awareness as the Deeper Self. It is who we are. It is our innate nature. It is our behavioral DNA imprint combined with our social imprint. It is connected to our protected life in the womb floating securely in amniotic fluid, and influenced by our life outside the instant we are thrust into our new external environment.

A parent lovingly coos in our ear, I love you, while at the same time caressing us or holding us in their nurturing embrace—bedtime stories, singing, caring parents, loving siblings, teachers, doting grandparents—the panoply of the idyllic *Golden Book* version of childhood round out the picture. Through this idealized portrait emerges the idealized Self—Da Vinci's term is Vitruvian man—perfection. In this storybook version, we all have stellar self-esteem and abundant self-confidence. We are respectful and caring in our daily discourse and interactions, and the like. This scenario is so not true that it is insidious and harmful to believe in it. It is not possible to achieve, let alone sustain, perfection. Then, the other question is whose interpretation of perfection is it? If it is mine, what if yours is different—who is right?

A second reality is far harsher—normal? Parents, even if you are fortunate enough to come from a two-parent family, are not necessarily enlightened parents. Even though they may love you, they don't always show it. They may raise their voices and shout at you or each other. As an infant when you are in church, synagogue, temple, or mosque naturally expressing your Self, spontaneously sharing your instinctive "ga-ga" and "goo-goo," these may be immediately followed by "shh" from a loved one. Clearly this shushing may not be meant as a rebuke or designed to censor our natural expression. Rather, it may be meant to comfort. However, this global verbal behavior is part of our social DNA passed down from generation to generation. It is what we do and it does stifle us. It may at some level be meant to comfort but it also criticizes.

As infants and toddlers, part of our Self-discovery process is through our voice. We are developing ourselves, exploring, and expanding. Then an adult censors us, asks us to conform. Most of the time, this is not maliciously censoring a child, but censor we do. Other scenarios beyond this are part of our daily reality as we grow. As the journey continues, we may be occasionally teased and taunted by other children. Teachers can threaten or intimidate, and, of course, many other factors influence our development.

We are not our behaviors.

Until we reach adulthood and we believe we have chosen to communicate as we do, to represent ourselves as we do. Whereas, in point of fact, we abdicated before the journey actually began. We unconsciously gave over control of ourselves and lost our autonomy—our sense of sovereignty. In addition, nowhere along the way, did we necessarily stop and determine, this is how I want to be known. Rarely do we stop along the way and say to anyone, "No longer will you have dominion over me."

Teaching discipline and respect are cornerstones of any civilized society. Silence can be golden. In a few paragraphs, I am painting with a broad brush stroke to make a point we don't often think about—the impact that voice and body language in all their manifestations—from parents to children, teachers to students, peer to peer, us to ourselves—frame who we become. How we speak and how we interact with one another does matter. Social imprinting is part of the human condition. But there comes a point when we recognize that we actually have a choice as to how we want to be known—and the first step in putting the puzzle pieces together is to ask ourselves, *How do I want to be known to my Self?*

The goal is not necessarily to do it better, but to do it more mindfully. Through awareness we create the opportunity to make informed choices. If we are not aware of our circumstances, we cannot change or enhance the situation in any way. Think about it. How many times a day do you let your behavior run you rather than you run your behavior? Whether in business or social settings, how often do you doubt yourself, seek approval, are afraid to claim an idea? Do you worry about what others might think; are you concerned about sounding too arrogant? Where did this lack of confidence and identity challenge begin? Metaphorically speaking, it began with "shh" and was then perpetuated in many other ways explicitly or implicitly. Through this Work, you will recognize that every single thing in life revolves around two things—to choose or not to choose. Even in abdication we make a choice by walking away. In Vocal Awareness, the goal is to make empowered choices. This is not arrogant, egotistical, inappropriately aggressive, or destructive in any way. It is primal. It is respectful of Self. Through informed and conscientious choice, we are less fragile, afraid, or inhibited, and therefore, our daily interactions are more congruent and less territorial. Communication Mastery offers a very distinct choice that enables us to create new patterns—informed, practiced, courageous, *conscious choices*.

> **Every single thing in life revolves around two things—to choose or not to choose. Even in abdication we make a choice by walking away. In Vocal Awareness, the goal is to make empowered choices.**

Vocal Awareness—Voice Is Who We Are

Communication Mastery is an outgrowth of Vocal Awareness. Vocal Awareness is the roots of the tree and its circulatory system. It nourishes who we are and everything we do. Communication Mastery is the flowering of the tree—the results that come from patient care and consistent effort.

Vocal Awareness informs everything we do. It supports us in living life to the best of our ability on our terms. It is the most comprehensive personal development work there is. It is also the most personal, and therein lies both the opportunity and the challenge. The opportunity is discovering, defining, practicing, and sustaining what it takes to be our best. The challenge is believing that we have what it takes to be that—our best.

Vocal Awareness is a very personal work. It is an intimate work. Please note that the root of the word intimate, *intimus* in part means *intrinsic* or *essential*. It is intrinsic to be who we are, essential that we must be who we are.

A number of years ago while teaching a corporate client who was quite conflicted about how bold he could actually be in a presentation we were preparing, I began discussing the concept of *hubris*. After looking it up in the dictionary, he discovered that the first definition was "extreme arrogance or an example of it." The following conversation ensued. I rhetorically said, "If you asked my former student Arnold Schwarzenegger what he thought about his body in his prime, for him to say anything other than the obvious, that is, 'I worked very hard to develop my muscles to their fullest and to define my body to look like this and achieve the success I have' would be foolish. If you asked Emmitt Smith, another former client, if he thought it arrogant as he began his NFL career to boldly state to himself and write down in his journal that he wanted to become the all-time leading rusher in the history of football, would he consider this arrogant? Emmitt would say, 'No.' I then asked, 'Why is it acceptable for these men to speak their truth about themselves and make bold statements about their vision, yet you are intimidated to confidently express your ideas to the CEO and to the Board in this important address when you are already seen as a significant leader in the company?' Use your strong resonant voice and definitively and confidently convey what it is you are there to say. This is not egotistical; it is professionally responsible, and who you are. You are the executive vice president of your division. You told me that this presentation creates a career opportunity for potential advancement—paving the way to ultimately becoming the CEO. It is your responsibility to yourself and the corporation to step in and step up."

It was at this moment that Vocal Awareness reframed for this leader the concept of *hubris*. He implicitly understood that in Vocal Awareness, *hubris* is not interpreted as extreme arrogance, rather, it acknowledges our understanding of excellence and what it takes to be our best irrespective of what anyone else might think. A few moments later, when he returned to work on his presentation on camera, there was a fundamental shift in what he embodied and how he communicated his message. He later reviewed his video at home and called me to say, "Thank you for helping me be myself." He is now one of the top five leaders of this worldwide company. Many consider him the heir apparent to the CEO.

Action Step ·········➤

Please create a communication journal. This journal is as personal as a diary. You may wish to track it on your computer, but my preference is a hardbound journal that will eventually encapsulate everything. Fill your communication journal with creative ideas, dreams, goals, anecdotes, clippings, images that support your vision for your personal and professional life—anything that inspires or helps you develop and sustain your commitment to being your best and to your emerging sense of Self.

2

COMMUNICATION MASTERY: THE JOURNEY CONTINUES

The man whom God loves is the onion with a million skins.
—Henry Miller

Vocal Awareness is not merely a performance-based skill, competitive skill, or a spiritual practice isolated to 20 minutes-a-day of saying a mantra. It is all of that, but so much more. Yes, of course, voice/communication is performance-based. We use our voices in performance when we deliver the ubiquitous PowerPoint presentation—on job interviews, at board meetings, media events, teleconferences, sales and marketing calls, classrooms, and the like. These are obvious moments in our daily lives when communication is performance-based. We are being evaluated. We succeed or fail because of how we are judged in these situations. Yes, we use voice competitively when, for example, we stand up for ourselves, spearhead an initiative, seek a promotion, strive to influence, or lead an organization. But we also have a spiritual relationship with our voices. Here, I refer in part to our inner voice as well as the internal dialogue that only we hear. This voice can encourage or suppress, sow seeds of doubt and distrust, or imbue us with inspiring drive and belief in ourselves. This voice can never be isolated, subjugated, or disregarded, but it can be tamed, adapted, and integrated to serve our needs.

Communication Mastery enables us to mobilize and utilize the full range of what is truly possible when we speak about voice. It equips us with consummate techniques and compassionate understanding. It arms us with strategic tools and enhances not just what we do but who we are, at all times respecting and reflecting *intrapersonal* communication in each *interpersonal* conversation. Intrapersonal communication influences everything and refers to the internal discourse—positive/negative, conscious/unconscious—that takes place within each of us. It is reflected through our behaviors, unresolved thoughts, body language, fears, doubts, failures, or successes. The sum total of who we are—our very essence—is *always* conveyed overtly and subliminally, both *verbally and nonverbally*, everywhere we go, in everything we do. Interpersonal communication obviously refers to our communication with one another, again both verbal and nonverbal. *Our voice is who we are.*

At this writing, it has been nearly 50 years since I created Vocal Awareness. During that time, I have been privileged to work with men and women from all walks of life and virtually every strata of the business world domestically and internationally—from entry-level employees to department heads, managers to executive vice presidents, CFOs, COOs, and board chairmen. At every level, the step-by-step Vocal Awareness Method has successfully equipped these individuals with the tools required for Communication Mastery. Throughout my career, one compelling truth is consistent around the globe: *In each seminar, management training program, one-on-one session, whether someone is stunningly successful or has just begun—the journey invariably begins the same way. We establish a goal, discover the fortitude required to achieve it, confront obstacles personal and professional, awaken to the awe of what is possible. Ultimately, if we truly commit to this level of excellence, the question I am invariably asked or we ask ourselves is one we must confront. As one of the foremost actors of our time inquired of me in a note many years ago: "Can I do this?" My answer was, as it always is, "Yes."*

This highly personal discovery and exploration, albeit unique to each and every one of us, is part of the human condition. There are inescapable features believed to be inherent to virtually each and every one of us— striving for achievement, gratification, curiosity, fear, doubt, and numerous others. These features are not necessarily dependent on gender, race, or class. No matter our situation in life, *we all want to better ourselves*. In Vocal Awareness/Communication Mastery, we all go through the same steps to discover our voice and uncover what it takes to be ourselves, no matter what our job title or professional responsibility may be.

A prominent CEO, clearly professionally confident, asked during a session with regard to her public presentations in contrast to those in-house, "Why do they want to hear what I have to say?" Another client, the president of an investment firm with a master's degree in finance, began working with me after 25 years in business with his father. His challenge was not simply feeling inadequate alongside his father when making investment decisions for clients worth hundreds of thousands or millions of dollars, but rather it was claiming his identity as a consummate business leader and problem solver. Another client who comes to mind, the highest-ranking woman—fourth in command in the multinational corporation she worked for—never felt as though she was respected as an equal among men.

In these three examples out of thousands, Vocal Awareness provided structure and clarity. It taught them how to resolve internal turmoil that had been perceived by them and others as longstanding, irrevocable character traits. Through the Work, they each began to recognize that change was possible and with their zeal, commitment, and follow-through—inevitable. To the best of their ability, each client followed the Vocal Awareness guidelines for Communication Mastery you will be exposed to in this book. Whether it was writing out goals, recording practice sessions, or doing vocal exercises to strengthen their voices and enhance their communication brands—everyone followed the same regimen. Ultimately, each leader maximized their communication ability, personally and professionally. Most important, *the same person showed up everywhere.*

It is not just what we say but how we say it.
Everything matters.

Another understanding implicit to success at any level in any discipline, but rarely discussed, is the recognition that *success requires risk*. The risk may be physical or emotional. The other day I was speaking with a great retired football player who, when he was a quarterback, took his team to victory in the Super Bowl. Personally he is a modest and confident man who always let his game speak for him. As a public speaker, he is now learning to speak for himself. In this particular lesson, we were vocalizing—warming up his voice—as we had been doing for some time. In preparation for a large public event, I was pushing the envelope for him to be bigger, louder, more authoritative; speak with greater resonance and strength than he usually would; and, at the same time, maintain his earnest and authentic brand (in Vocal Awareness—his Persona). He records every lesson on his iPhone so we can play it back and review. This simple technique has been instrumental in his gaining communication confidence as listening to the recording enables him to hear what others hear. In this lesson he was particularly astonished at how loud he sounded in the room and how much physical effort and awareness it took him to sustain his voice and delivery. Before listening back he said, "My voice sounds and feels unnatural." What sounded loud and aggressive in the room and felt physically effortful, was not that at all. When he heard the recording, he experienced a naturally authoritative, charismatic, and confident leader. I rhetorically commented: *"It is amazing how much work it takes to be ourselves in public."* As we began to conclude our session, I discussed the notion of what I call Comfort Zones. I said, "For years your comfort zone was being a great athlete. That is what you knew. You were never intimidated to play football. You could take a hit, deliver one, block, be tackled, pass a football 60 yards and do it all astoundingly well in a matter of moments. This was your comfort zone. Public speaking and singing are mine. I could never envision doing what you did. But, if I ever wanted to, I would have to do what it took to overcome my trepidation. If I aspired to play football and you were my teacher, you would patiently and steadfastly teach me to do what was required to play the game. You are now learning to do something you have never done, which has taken you out of your comfort zone. You came to me to become a public speaker, and I am your teacher helping you navigate the terrain to inhabit a new comfort zone so that you can be your best in the speaking field as you were on the football field." Later that day when he delivered his remarks, the positive feedback was overwhelming. Friends and colleagues consistently acknowledged his authenticity, intellectual insight, and ease. One close friend confided, that he sounded more intelligent. Yet, all he had done was follow the principles you are about to discover.

One of the true joys of this work is to help the people I work with fulfill their dreams. Yes, some people are smarter or work intrinsically harder than others just as some people are natural singers or faster runners. Those are gifts. Even if we don't have a gift, however, we all have a talent. Part of my responsibility is to help you recognize your talent and do whatever it takes to fulfill it. A couple of years ago a gentleman in his mid-forties came to study with me. He had just sold a very successful, third generation, family-owned company. Virtually all his life he was groomed to be a business leader. Once in retirement, he discovered he was bored. In casting about for what he might do next, he surfed the Internet and discovered my website. He sent me an e-mail, and he made his first appointment when we spoke. Within the next year, what emerged was the fulfillment of his inner voice creating a new career path and entrepreneurial profession. He is now a psychologist and life coach, and he leads couples retreats around the country. He creates online courses, records content in his home studio, and leads public workshops.

As we transitioned from one comfort zone to another, we began with the familiar and crafted a business plan. Instead of a plan designed to support a brick-and-mortar business, I morphed it into a personal business plan designed to help him fulfill his vision. It had the same timelines and deliverables he had used for years in business, but we substituted ideas for numbers. As he had strategized five years out for his company and his hundreds of employees, he now did the same for himself and his future employees. With the emergence of his inner voice, he also began to manifest a more nuanced speaking voice calibrated to reflect who he was—genuine, warm, and sincere. His voice also developed a nurturing sonorous richness. He taught and counseled with a comfortable, relaxed cadence.

Vocal Awareness/Communication Mastery is an integrative Work. It is cognizant of the intrinsic themes experienced by all of us as we traverse the peaks and valleys of the human condition. In committing to this Work, you are committing to be your best, not merely through what you do, but in who you are.

Before moving on and continuing the discussion of the commonalities of what it takes to be a successful business leader, one of the goals of this book is to shed light on the role emotions and behavior play—the ebb and flow of fear and doubt, confidence and belief—and how they impact each of us as we strive to improve ourselves. To do so it is imperative to identify one additional bump in the road that may appear as an insurmountable obstacle on your path, but as you acquire the skills of Communication Mastery, this "roadblock" can eventually vanish altogether. To be your best requires uncovering, confronting, and coping with the irrational fears that reside within you. They lurk in the deep recesses in all of us to such a degree that we actually believe they are an irrevocable part of who we are rather than emotional vestigial remains, shadows that, when light is cast upon them, vanish. These fears are part of the behavioral aspects of the human condition. It is imperative that all leaders recognize that the fear that may impact or impede you affects not only you but your company, your management team, your constituents, shareholders, the public—everyone in your sphere of influence. For all of us who dedicate ourselves to mastery in any form, we recognize that irrational fears can be surmounted. Instead of seeing these fears as negative and immutable, we see them as positive and transformative.

Mastery allows and requires my passion to be deliberate and consciously meaningful in my life. Through Mastery, I create the opportunity to be more meaningful to others.

"The Greatest Fear"

For generations, there has been no greater presumed sociological fear than the fear of public speaking. There is even a word for it "glossophobia." It comes from the Greek words *glossa* meaning "tongue" and *phobas* meaning "fear or dread." The comedian Jerry Seinfeld once joked that almost everyone attending a funeral would rather be the deceased than the one delivering the eulogy. A senior executive in a Fortune 100 company I consult with once said to me, "If I had known you 20 years ago, I would be running the company now, but my fear of public speaking was so severe that I was unable to take advantage of certain career opportunities because they required me to be a consummate public speaker." Have you ever experienced cotton mouth, moments when your voice or body trembles, or you heavily perspire or blush when anticipating having to speak in any public context—from a job interview to a major public event? It can happen anywhere, to anyone—panic attacks when anticipating a conversation with superiors in your corporate structure or first-time meetings, butterflies in the pit of your stomach or sweaty palms when you were a student in the classroom afraid to be called upon or when preparing to go out on a date. We have all, at one time or another, been impaled on the emotional point of this devastating spear, and we have been led to believe there is likely nothing we can do about it. The conclusion derived is that public speaking is our greatest fear. This old axiom is a simplistic misnomer, and as with all "simple" statements we accept it as fact and don't look any deeper. You are about to learn public speaking *is not* our greatest fear.

The Two Greatest Fears

There are two fears: fear of abandonment and fear of our own greatness, ownership of our power.

The first is fear of abandonment. In our daily lives, every time we wonder what someone is thinking about us when we speak or when that person questions what we say when we say it, we are abandoning our Selves. Since no one can read our mind, nor can we read anyone else's, we never have an answer. The physical response to this fear of abandonment is that we hold our breath, perhaps look away, our blood pressure rises, and our body tenses. In addition, this insidious trait of abandonment gives others dominion over us and, by extension, prevents us from overcoming this conditioned response.

The second is fear of our own greatness, ownership of our power. To own our power is to *be who we are*. In this context, power is not aggressive or domineering, rather it is to be *sovereign*. "Supreme excellence or an example of it" is at the root of this word. Notice *be who we are* does not say *present who we are,* which implies seeking approval and/or permission of others. This fear of owning our power is negatively reflected in so many ways—speaking in a breathy manner; a high-pitched tone (especially for women); equivocal phrases such as "I think" or "I mean"; white noise such as "ums" and "uhs" that habitually permeate every conversation; avoiding eye contact when speaking to another or when not listening to another; and speaking too rapidly for fear of taking too much time are but a few examples.

With the clarity of your new understanding coupled with the principles and techniques you will learn in this book, you *will* be able to expunge all fear and claim your greatness.

If you can imagine it, you can engineer it.
—Walt Disney

One of my clients is a very prominent leader in one of the most successful multinational corporations in the world. His success for decades has been predicated on his expertise in his professional field. Sometime ago, when we met for the first time, he was exposed to the understanding that true mastery is not simply predicated on *what* you do but on *who* you are. As this Work unfolded and he became a more proficient and effective communicator, he achieved even greater success. One day, however, I received an urgent e-mail from him. When I called him back and we spoke, he candidly said, "I am afraid." I asked, "Afraid of what?" We talked around this for a few minutes, and what was revealed was his fear of finally confronting who he knew himself to be and being asked to embody it. His trepidation manifested as he recognized that he had no other course of action but to claim who he was. It was no longer only about the title on the door or the job description, but also about the responsibility to be seen for *who he is* not only for *what he does*. This evoked in him a feeling of anxiety and fear. It was at this moment I introduced a key Vocal Awareness maxim, *The same person shows up everywhere.* I went on to explain what I meant by this. Whether your role is as a business leader, husband, father, colleague—you speak with the same voice. When you're speaking at the PTA, across the boardroom table, or on the phone with a colleague, you obviously have no other voice to use but your own. In Vocal Awareness, we strive to discover, develop, integrate, and maximize our Vocal potential. Our goal is to embody and confidently reflect the same voice, the same person wherever we go, whatever we do. His understanding of this was so comforting and made everything very clear. This seemingly obvious recognition was epiphanal. He inhaled deeply, relaxed, and sighed. In that moment, he recognized there was nothing to fear. He wasn't required to be, nor could he be, more than he was. In fact, all he ever needed to do was to be himself. With Vocal Awareness, he was acquiring the tools to communicate even more consistently and confidently as *himself* in Communication Mastery at all times.

As our conversation continued, I asked him to be in the Work (a Vocal Awareness principle: to be and do our best). Before the end of our discussion, his internal compass was once again pointing due north, but with even greater clarity than moments earlier. As more was revealed to him, he discovered that more was possible. By doing the Work, he understood that his hand was confidently on the tiller, and he did have the skills to navigate the river not only when the current was flowing easily, but even in treacherous rapids. The question is: Is this an anomaly being pinioned to our own personal behaviors and tenuous belief systems? Of course not, this is true for all of us. At some point in our lives, we confront being ineffective, afraid, even emotionally immobilized. Beyond going into therapy, joining Toastmasters, finding a life coach or religious authority, or reading self-help books, we do not necessarily know what to do about this. Even if we find success through such resources, we are not necessarily once and for all solving the problem. This is because "We don't know what we don't know." There will always be vague or overt unresolved issues that never disappear.

By its very nature, all mastery is transformative Work. However, Communication Mastery is not simply mastery where the learning is skill-based, oriented around an exacting standard. In the "driver's manual" accompanying skill-based mastery, it is implicit that there is an on/off switch. We are only in mastery when we are dancing *Swan Lake*, running a 100-meter dash, singing a Bach cantata, or perhaps on a profound religious or spiritual path when in prayer or meditation. *Communication Mastery is not only mastering one's prowess as a great communicator, but it is also discovering how to be and do something in a profoundly committed way and there is no on/off switch*. In this case, it is the commitment to live life to the best of your ability on your terms, as well as to communicate integrally and masterfully at all times, not only when you are doing what you do but when being who you are. This is the key to success in business—in life. It is trainable.

In *The Tropic of Capricorn*, Henry Miller wrote:

> *The man whom God loves is the onion with a million skins. To shed the first layer is painful beyond words; the next layer is less painful, the next still less, until finally the pain becomes pleasurable, more and more pleasurable, a delight, an ecstasy. And then*

there is neither pleasure nor pain, but simply darkness yielding before the light. And as the darkness falls away the wound comes out of its hiding place: the wound which is man, man's love, is bathed in light. The identity which was lost is recovered. Man walks forth from his open wound, from the grave which he had carried about with him so long.[1]

This stunning visual insight evokes a piquant truth rarely examined. The dedicated effort and ceaseless commitment required to passionately pursue, not self-discovery, but discovery of Self.

In a recent Vocal Awareness seminar, one of the most moving experiences was observing the astonished faces, the deep emotion reflected through tears, laughter, a hug, and subsequent e-mail, from one of the participants around the simple discovery: "I never knew this was possible. I never knew that I could actually speak better or feel more confident and consciously communicate in a way that not only reflected my confidence or my eloquence but, more important, embodied in a truly integral and integrative way what I had only previously admitted to myself—this is how I wanted to be known."

From Presentation to Performance

Traditionally, we are taught to *present*. It begins benignly enough in our childhoods—from the dinner table to a middle school history class presentation to going on our first date, then it extends to applying to college, interviewing for our first job, and beyond. The pattern is unconsciously established. To get what we want in life, we have to be approved of by others. When we present, we implicitly seek acceptance. This acceptance is not just of what we say, but implicitly of who we are when we say it. We want parental approval, a good grade, admission to college, a job. Without even recognizing it, we have established unconscious patterns of submission to the dictates of others. To *achieve* our goal, we *present* what we *think* others want to see. We have been encoded—good behavior = desired outcome. Of course, there are social norms. But the ignominious reality is, we stop exploring who we are capable of *being* and unconsciously settle for presenting how we think we are supposed to be in order to be accepted. Unbeknownst to each of us, we have ceded our destiny. To reclaim our birthright, our personal sovereignty, requires learning to *be* who we are and no longer *present* who we are. This is where Communication Mastery becomes indispensable.

Performance

Performance is a word that people in business have occasionally had a challenge with truly understanding. Many think performance only has a theatrical connotation, most commonly referring to performing on stage. *Every public encounter is a performance because someone is watching.* How do we *perform* authentically? How do we genuinely and comfortably simply represent our Selves as we choose to be, and not inauthentically present in an unconscious, habituated way? As speech is habit, speaking is unconscious. Even when we have rehearsed, we do not think about the sounds, nor are we cognizant of the articulation of the words themselves. As the Vocal Awareness axiom reminds us, "We don't realize how much work it takes *to be* our Selves while someone is watching." This admonition doesn't apply solely to critical moments (i.e., business meetings, job interviews, or PowerPoint presentations) but in everyday conversation, which is where the majority of our life is lived. In the Old French, the word *parfounir* in part means *accomplish*. Another connection is to the word *forme*, meaning literally *form*.[2] So, when we *perform*, we accomplish something. In this Work, we learn what it takes to be our Selves, to accomplish that task, and to fulfill that possibility at all times.

Vocal Awareness is not only a vocal method. It is that—and consummately so. It is also an elegantly simple, gently commanding system for living life in full *Conscious Awareness*.

What may on the face of this page seem complicated is not. In fact, Vocal Awareness and Communication Mastery become quite simple in a matter of hours. As we create bullets and text for a PowerPoint presentation, prepare for a job interview, put on a headset to answer the phone at work, engage in online teleconferencing or videoconferencing, and even while nonverbally communicating sitting at our computers typing, we are learning *to hear our Voice, listen to our Voice, see the words* we are thinking and speaking and all along *tuning in* and no longer allowing ourselves to *tune out*.

Ask yourself: Do I like my voice? Do I like what I sound like? Am I comfortable communicating in every context—personal and professional? Then ask yourself what qualities you don't like and why. Two definitions for the word *voice* are: "sound produced by the vocal organs of a vertebrate, especially a human" and "the sound by a human being using the vocal folds for talking, singing, laughing, crying, screaming, and other controlled sounds emanating from the mouth."[3] Clearly these definitions do not illuminate an understanding of what *Voice* truly is. Does it help to know that it comes from the Latin *vox* meaning "voice," or that it is related to the Latin *vocare*—the call, the calling? Does it help to know that the vocal folds merely stretch and vibrate, and the sound they produce is only produced through the air in the lungs pushed out via the abdominal muscles? That doesn't help either.

In other words, empirical information alone does not enhance one's ability to communicate or speak better. Rather, answer this question: Would I like to be able to fulfill my life's ambition? Would I like to be able to speak and communicate confidently and effectively in every situation with no stress or fear?

If the answer is yes, then the next question is: Do I believe this is even possible? An absolute, unequivocal *Yes!* is my answer. That is Communication Mastery. The *Voice* that is the subject of this book, in the Vocal Awareness Method, is not a vocal system designed solely to train a better speaking voice (though one can gain an extraordinary speaking voice even if the sound is already as eloquent as the greatest Shakespearean actor), but Vocal Awareness is a vocal system. Vocal Awareness integrates mind/body/spirit and integrates the *inner* Voice through the *outer* voice—consciously, strategically, effectively in everything that is said and done, even in the way we walk, sit, stand, look at one another, or just breathe. It is mastery. This is no different from any other discipline where mastery in that discipline is achieved. However, in every other walk of life where mastery is the pursuit, we do not settle for sort of, but rather each one of us strives to always serve the Work, serve the goal, and learn the skills to be the very best we can be in our chosen fields.

Vocal Awareness begins with accepting the premise that fulfilling our vision, fulfilling our calling is actually possible and, then, committing to doing what it takes every day in the office, every day at our job—no matter what it is, no matter age, social status, or job status—whether a PBX operator or the chairman of the company. *Voice* is the equalizer.

Communication Mastery Is a Choice

In any discipline, the only way one can achieve mastery is to work hard—very, very hard. Until this Work, mastery has been achieved only in a specific skill or discipline. On the athletic field, for example, competition is the norm. Everyone has to have a certain level of development to even play the game. If one chooses to be a great artist or a great athlete, the way is clear. We find a teacher or a coach, and we are taught our skill. We are taught everything—from the most basic to the most advanced techniques. We study minute details; our practice is supervised for years; we watch our performances captured on video; we are taught how to overcome fear and disappointment, be victorious. In public discourse, this understanding of what it takes to be our best has never existed—until now.

Singers are taught how to breathe, how to support their tone, to express their musical aesthetic. A ballet dancer learns proper technique and applies this knowledge to the art of dance. Athletes are taught how to properly stretch, how to kick a ball, throw, run, and leap. Before artists and athletes are deemed professional, they have spent years mastering their crafts.

In business the skills of the trade are learned as well. MBAs are required for certain positions; consummate IT ability, accounting, or marketing training for others. After mastering given requisite skill sets, the unspoken premise is that one is a professional.

Company sales directives often state, "Speak persuasively. Speak confidently." Part of a company mission may be to communicate with one voice.

However, we simply give talks from bullets, we speak too fast when nervous, our pitch rises when we are anxious, or we don't make eye contact with another person when speaking to them. All this is the norm—not an anomaly. Frankly, we are not taught the basic communication skills required to be as successful as possible—how to verbally and masterfully communicate our message with the same degree of refinement and understanding that is a prerequisite for true professionalism in any other endeavor. It is only in public speaking, from the most basic to the most substantial, where our unconscious behaviors—our habits—are allowed to negatively impact our performance. A dancer who cannot do chaines to the left will not have a career. A baseball player who can't hit a curve ball will not make it to the major leagues. Yet, in our highly competitive societies, a business professional or a political leader who cannot communicate effectively still has a job. It may not matter that one is socially awkward or speaks too rapidly and thus appears uncomfortable. As a society, each of us in our day-to-day interactions accepts this ineffective communication style. In a word, we *settle* for it because we don't know we have a choice. Even if you have taken sales or leadership training courses, rest assured, you have never learned how to be masterfully persuasive, masterfully confident, and masterfully yourself in all situations. Communication Mastery is the how. As previously stated, there has always been an implicit assumption that because we know how to speak, we know how to communicate. This is the tragic flaw.

There are business coaches who teach business principles, whether it's in the model of Peter Drucker or the Japanese business model Kaizen. Even the late Stephen Covey referenced *voice* as the eighth habit, referring to the inner voice, not our speaking voice. There are significant thought leaders from Joseph Campbell to Malcolm Gladwell, motivational speakers such as Tony Robbins, spiritual guides from Deepak Chopra to Thich Nhat Hanh, coaches, media trainers, and other consultants who all have a piece of the pie. In business/life, there has been no clear-cut method that teaches us how to take lessons from these and other master teachers and implement them in our daily dialogue. Communication Mastery does this. It teaches us how. As you will learn, it also teaches "the same person shows up everywhere"—not one communication style at work and one at home. In Vocal Awareness there is no on/off switch.

> *You must dedicate your life to mastering your work.*
> *That is the secret of success.*
> —Jiro Ono

> *Insist on yourself. Never imitate.*
> —Ralph Waldo Emerson

I recently worked with the senior leadership of a global corporation in preparation for two significant annual meetings. The training included everyone from the chairman and the head of HR to director-level employees. As our Vocal Awareness training got under way, with the exception of the chairman who had been a long-time client, no one else had been exposed to Vocal Awareness. The preparation window for our first meeting was very brief. It began on a Thursday and presentations were on Monday. For the second event, preparation began a week-and-a-half out on Skype and concluded in person over two days prior to their second presentation. The abilities ranged from seasoned individuals to those who were very raw in communicating in large public settings. Regardless of whether they were beginners or seasoned public speakers, no one understood the question, What is your communication brand? or How do you want to be known as a presenter? No one was aware of the necessary elements required to deliver a message as effectively as possible. By effective, I'm referring to proper breathing techniques, how to tell a story rather than merely convey data, the significance of body language, the importance of changing pace in delivery, volume, pitch, and so on. They had no concept of what it takes to be an effective communicator, let alone a consummate communicator. Wherever I travel and teach in business settings—Latin America to the United States, Asia to Europe—it is never any different. For a performing artist or an athlete, this would never be the case. Knowing the basics is entry level for ultimate success.

In the first of the following two situations, an individual, prior to his presentation, was as nervous as I've ever observed anyone before. Because I had earned the employee's trust over the first few days, I could be direct while being supportive and caring, and I reminded the executive how to use the principles he had learned. The subsequent presentation was superb. The senior vice president was no longer self-conscious and fearful, but rather conscious of Self. He came off the stage and actually said, "That was fun!"

A number of years ago during a workshop at the Aspen Institute in Aspen, Colorado, I taught a participant a couple of basic Vocal Awareness exercises. Following the exercises, when she resumed speaking in front of the group, they were stunned at the change in her voice. I said, "Paradoxically, the change in her voice was of less interest to me. It has to change. She just warmed up. What is of greater interest to me is how your perception of the woman changed."

These examples illustrate how the application of Vocal Awareness principles quickly and effectively changes how we play the game. Communication Mastery is designed to no longer allow us to simply present in an unconscious, inconsistent manner revealing our personal discomfort, anxiety, and inadequacies—this is only habit. Rather, as in the arts and athletics, the discovery is that *structure does not impinge; it liberates. Freedom without direction is chaos.* As we begin to understand the Vocal Awareness paradigm and adhere to its fundamental tenets, the structure supports us through disciplined practice. In this Work, we no longer reveal what we don't want people to see but instead claim only what we want people to know. In today's competitive global marketplace and challenging economic times, Communication Mastery is the advantage. It is the way to maximize *every* encounter, *every* business opportunity as effectively as possible.

We have heard the adage, "People do business with people they like." Communication Mastery teaches us not simply how to put our best foot forward— presenting ourselves—but rather *to be* ourselves in full Conscious Awareness, always recognizing that it is not just the *message* but the *messenger* that matters. *The same person shows up everywhere.*

Conscious Awareness

Several years ago while consulting over a long period of time with a Fortune 100 company, I was training, among others, one of the senior leaders of the company. As president of the organization's largest division, this individual was responsible for overseeing about a billion dollars of business. In college she was an All-American basketball player. When we began working together, she was in her late thirties and still played league basketball on the weekends. During a session, she told me a story about one weekend when a man was harassing her from the sidelines. He was incessant, and it went on for some time. More than once she told him to be quiet. He wouldn't do it. As a last resort, she threw the basketball at him full force, hitting him in the chest and knocking him down. When he got up, he came over and decked her with his fist. She never backed down. The point is she had no fear of confrontation.

One of the reasons we were working together was because she had a professional challenge with a male subordinate on her staff who would not respect her leadership, and she always backed down. Basically she lacked confidence in dealing with him, was ineffective, and appeared insecure. This was the same woman who was competitive and driven on the court, but when in meetings with this individual, she behaved as though she had left her tennis shoes in the locker room. She spoke rapidly, developed a nervous blinking habit, and, most interestingly, raised the pitch of her voice and averted eye contact. We spent approximately three months orchestrating the day she would fire him. We worked on all her professional skills and talents, which helped her understand how to integrate them in full *Conscious Awareness* as a communicator/leader in business. She noted that our drills and study reminded her of everything she did to develop as a great collegiate basketball player—establishing her identity—clarifying her role as a player which included her responsibility to herself and her teammates; developing a belief system; goal setting; exercising daily and the like. In this regard, as she did stretches and drills during every basketball practice, our sessions began with vocal exercises to warm up and strengthen her voice. (You will thoroughly study and practice these exercises in Chapter 4.) To help her identify her brand as a business leader, she crafted a Persona Statement—the template that helped her recognize how she wanted to be known professionally. (This concept is fully developed in Chapter 3.) Note: At this preliminary point in our narrative, it is less important that you understand the details of what you will come to know as the Work and more important that you have a conceptual understanding of the developmental process.

Continuing, as with all my clients, we videotaped our lessons. This simple process enabled her to objectify a very subjective experience. When I would replay a moment from the video during her lessons, it helped clarify what I had been teaching and also helped her better understand what she was doing—both successfully or less successfully. In addition, she was able to review our sessions at a later time, which enabled her to practice more effectively. Another strategic learning opportunity was role playing. We visualized and staged the moment of the impending meeting with me in the guise of her employee while she role played her leadership moment. We also practiced the dialogue we had created, which helped her gain confidence and appear more natural in each and every run through. This calls to mind once again, the following statement which will be repeated throughout this book. It is *so* fundamental yet always overlooked: *We do not realize how much work it takes to be ourselves in public.* This is a reiteration with a subtle shift of an earlier statement in this chapter, "The same person shows up everywhere."

The time for the scheduled 9 a.m. meeting arrived. The subordinate was gone before the end of business that day. Part of the point of this story is to call into question the oft-used business adage, "It's not personal." It is *always* personal.

As already stated, the way we speak, the way we communicate with one another is not who we are but ingrained patterns—unconscious behaviors—habit. Conscious Awareness helps us discover these old patterns and discard them. In their place, we construct new patterns that become the scaffold that effectively support mind/body/spirit integration—Communication Mastery.

Another story that comes to mind is about an athlete who is considered to be one of the greatest players in the history of football. We were working recently when he interrupted an exercise he was doing and said, "This is hard work." I asked, "Did you ever say that one time in all the years you played professional football?" He sheepishly replied "No." "Then, you can't say it here. The same person/the same champion shows up everywhere. The same discipline it took to be one of the greatest players in football is required in your new endeavor as a public speaker/broadcaster/advocate." He returned to the exercise and now more clearly understands the consistent dedication required to be his best, not only on the gridiron but in life. This is true for all of us—sustaining the effort is a prerequisite for excellence.

Champions Do It Differently

*If you believe in yourself, have dedication and pride, and never quit,
you will be a Champion. The price of victory is high,
but so are the rewards.*

—Paul "Bear" Bryant

I have had the privilege of teaching a myriad of world-class athletes—Olympic champions and Hall of Famers in sports from football, basketball, baseball, soccer, track and field, swimming, gymnastics, and motocross and supercross. Through the prism of working with elite athletes for so many years, except in rare instances where there is truly an extraordinary gift, I've observed that the only difference between an average or even a very good athlete and a champion is that a champion works harder and smarter and is more focused, dedicated, and committed to *always* being his or her best. Champions do not "take a down off."

In 2007, I helped former Dallas Cowboy wide receiver, my dear friend and longtime student, Michael Irvin craft and deliver his National Football League Hall of Fame acceptance speech. The ceremonies took place on an elaborate outdoor stage on the adjacent football field in Canton, Ohio. Vocal Awareness/Communication Mastery understands that to become our best not just in what we do but in who we are, requires a belief system, a game plan, a respect for risk, a recognition of failure, and the occasional defeat. It also teaches us how to stand up after getting knocked down to continue our journey. Michael and I began developing his speech a month to the day prior to his induction ceremony. Our goal was for him to deliver his speech fully memorized and fully embodied, but we were still tweaking it at 11 p.m. the night before the ceremony. The day of the enshrinement, Michael had been on stage for a couple of hours while other champions were being recognized. We huddled offstage for about 15 minutes before he was to speak and I asked, "Are you sure you don't need any notes?" He said, "No buddy—I committed it to spirit." Michael was impeccable. Not only were the words memorized, but he epitomized not only a sports champion, but a champion who transcends sports. His speech, now recognized in many surveys as one of the greatest sports speeches of all time, concluded with a memorable line reflecting not just what it takes to be a sports hero, but what it takes to succeed in life: "At that moment a voice came over me and said, 'Look up, get up, and don't ever give up!' You tell everyone or anyone that has ever doubted, thought they did not measure up, or wanted to quit, you tell them to look up, get up, and don't ever give up!"

Following Michael's induction, in 2010 and 2011, I was honored to help and support Emmitt Smith and Marshall Faulk with their respective Hall of Fame induction speeches. Emmitt and I worked 100-plus hours on a 22-minute speech that was also fully memorized. Following a downpour prior to Marshall's enshrinement, I spent 90 minutes inputting his speech on the teleprompter and annotating it in Vocal Awareness (you will learn this technique in Chapter 6). Like Michael, their performance goal was not to embody a football champion but a champion that transcends football. They definitely succeeded!

Athletes and business leaders are similar. They are highly motivated, goal-oriented, and work very hard. One of the first things I say to every athlete I work with is, "You brought the gift to the sport, but someone taught you to do every single thing you do." In business, we bring our expertise to the workplace but communicating that expertise is not one of those learned skills, nor is it for athletes. In sports, athletes study game film. They watch their performance and study their opponents hour upon hour. In Communication Mastery, I employ the same regimen. We study *game film*. We record conversations and public presentations, and then we go back and view, listen to, and study them. We record our Vocal Awareness sessions—again, our game film. In part this enables us to objectify—to step back and observe ourselves becoming aware of what we are doing and how we are doing it, what we are saying and how we are saying it.

The following story is a microcosm of many first lessons. It is designed for you to walk in the client's shoes and experience the unfolding of a first lesson. Again, at this point, it is less important that you understand the details, as they will be fully explained in the next two chapters. Perhaps as you read his story, you may even occasionally stop along the way to practice with him.

Some time ago I consulted with a prominent real estate corporation. Initially, I worked with the founder/chairman. He then asked me to work with his sales force and, ultimately, with the president of the company, who was at first exceedingly resistant. The president was a successful business leader, and a fine salesman, and he didn't believe he needed any help.

For our first session, there was a video camera set up to record his PowerPoint rehearsal. Throughout his career, his presentational style was to write down a few bullets on cards to support his slide presentation. Then with the bullets as a guide, he would extemporize and speak to the slide. After a few minutes, I stopped his run-through and asked him to write out the opening paragraph. When he finished I said, "Traditionally, you've done a fine job speaking to the slide. When you review in a moment, you will see that it may appear natural but you will also recognize that it is not polished and lacks originality. In addition, you will see that your narrative for the first three slides virtually duplicates what is already presented on the slides rather than amplifying the message." We then returned to the rehearsal process, this time reading the opening paragraph. When he finished, we stopped and reviewed. His first response was, "Even though I am reading, I notice that my voice is stronger, my pitch lower, and I somehow appear more confident and knowledgeable."

After that, I introduced two new Vocal Awareness principles. First I asked, "Feel what it might be like to embody a man of stature." (The Stature principle will be fully defined in Chapter 4.) He immediately noticed that he inhaled, opened his chest, and stood taller, and he said, "Somehow I feel more relaxed and centered at the same time." We repeated this a number of times.

Following the introduction of Stature, which is preparing for everything we do, I then introduced him to the first two Rituals—also both fully developed in Chapter 4. The 1st Ritual is Thank You to My Source and the 2nd Ritual is Love and Let Go. As he engaged the first two Rituals, once again the first thing he observed was that he inhaled and felt more relaxed and centered.

The third element for him was to notice how he breathed. I role played with him for a few minutes and demonstrated what it sounded like when he gasped for air. In addition, I helped him see that a short, tense breath affected how we visually saw him; that is, it made his tongue and jaw tighter, his body language tense, and his delivery more halting. Through this exploration, he also discovered that his breathing patterns were simply unconscious habits and that the short, tense breaths contributed to a higher-pitched voice and also made his delivery too fast.

We then worked on a Vocal Awareness breathing technique (again, fully developed in Chapter 4). With this technique, he discovered a subtle but significant difference between *taking* a breath and *allowing* a slow, *silent* breath. In Communication Mastery it is not simply the physical act of breathing that is paramount, but also the recognition that, at the highest levels of performance refinement, *breath is not only physical but also emotional*. In moments of stress (i.e., public presentations such as board and sales meetings, job interviews, and annual performance reviews when a positive outcome is not assured, and we may be feeling stressed, possibly traumatized, or lacking self-confidence), the first thing the body does is hold its breath. As you will discover, this *simple* technique can be a game changer. It will help you relax and take more time with your message.

The last element was the technique of How to Make Voice Visual (fully explored in Chapter 5). He wrote the word *Stature* at the top of the page, which reminded him to focus and separated him from his previous habitual behavior to a more performance-based awareness. He marked where to breathe, which created a better cadence (i.e., less rushed, a more natural delivery, and helped relax him). He underlined *key* words, which better enabled him to communicate the most important ideas.

We then went back with the camera rolling. As a conductor leads an orchestra, I visually guided him through his performance. This enabled him to tell the story more authentically and confidently. Finally, he presented the opening few minutes by himself—first taking a moment to focus. He then read in *Conscious Awareness* his annotated script. He was astonished at the difference. What he thought was going to sound canned or too studied was actually naturally poised and polished. He said, "It sounds like me." Again, extrapolating the Vocal Awareness axiom, we do not understand how much work it takes to *be ourselves* while someone is watching.

In the above story, please notice the way each element was incrementally introduced—not all at one time. This is very important. This step-by-step approach is fundamental to effective learning. Be mindful and respectful of what you must require of yourself to learn a new skill let alone, ultimately, master it. Patience, diligence, and attention to detail are the order of the day. Please focus on and understand each element before moving on.

The goal of this Work is *Empowerment Through Voice*. Communication Mastery is a *Being* work, but we have *to do to be*.

Action Step ··········➤

In your journal, note daily communication experiences—emerging awareness, observations and perceptions, including any relevant successes or challenges. You may also want to add notes, such as how your colleagues communicate. At this point, the purpose is simply to become aware of communication in ways you may never have cognitively noticed. Also, please begin to think about your brand—how you want to be known—and write it in your journal. At this point, bullets are OK (i.e., specific words such as strong, happy, earnest, intelligent, and so on). You will develop your brand concept later in the book.

3

SPIRITUAL PRAGMATISM: THE JOURNEY DEEPENS

There is consciousness here in the body. The whole living world is informed by consciousness. . . . Man should not submit to the powers from outside but command them. How to do it is the problem.

—Joseph Campbell, *The Power of Myth*

Spiritual Pragmatism is an evolutionary concept. Simply speaking, Spiritual Pragmatism integrates two seemingly unrelated concepts: *spiritual* having to do with our mental or intellectual nature and *pragmatism. Spiritual* is defined as "mental or intellectual armor" and *pragmatism* as the origin of which is connected to a "deed" or "to do" something. A pragmatist then is one who is practical rather than theoretical. There are, of course, schools of thought that teach philosophical or political pragmatism. Now, there is Spiritual Pragmatism that is the embodiment of the human spirit as a practical means for *Being Our Selves.* In Communication Mastery, *Spiritual Pragmatism enhances the communication of who we are.* It is a more complete understanding of what it takes to embody our

Selves. In Vocal Awareness/Communication Mastery this concept of identity is referred to as our *Deeper Self.*

I was recently teaching a woman who is a midlevel executive in her corporation. Jane is passionate, earnest, and exceptionally bright. She has been committed to this Work for some time. Following the presentation she and I had been working on, part of my analysis I shared with her was that she actually had a gift rather than just a skill or talent. Her gift was the ability to connect with others—her intrinsic insights and sensitivity were reflected in her leadership style and interpersonal skills. When she spoke with people one-on-one or in a large group, she intuitively connected to whomever she was speaking. This connection created enthusiastic responses from her colleagues. They trusted her and worked exceptionally hard because they knew she cared about them—not just about what they did, but about who they were. This observation intimidated her. I then went on to explain: "Visualize yourself as an artistic prodigy—for example, the violin virtuoso Sarah Chang's first meeting with a teacher as a child. The teacher immediately sees the prodigious talent as I see yours—the student's capacity. With this recognition, the training is now targeted and systematically developed day after day, year after year. However, you came to me midlife as a mature woman, and your talent, though not artistic, is intellectually evolved and astutely practical and is no less a gift than this great artist's. You have actually intuited this yourself for many years but didn't know how to address it. Now, through the prism of Spiritual Pragmatism, we are fleshing out the very essence of who you are. It is no longer only about how well you do your job, but equally about your accountability to Being who you are." Combining these two attributes is a formula for success for yourself and by extension, others.

Jane's response was palpable—deeply moving. Subsequently, she has had even greater success in the organization. She also now has the courage to begin laying plans to step out on her own—something she has dreamed about for years but never felt confident enough to do. She has created a mission statement and a one-year business plan.

Spiritual Pragmatism enabled this significant woman to understand how to claim the best of who she is. She learned how to confront and overcome the emotional and personal fragility of her daily life—the very act of being human—without silencing herself. She is learning how not to compartmentalize and "behave" in her habitually programmed way. Jane now respectfully acknowledges her Deeper Self, the very core of who she is through this Work, and is becoming stronger, more proficient, and even more human.

Persona Statement: Voice Is Identity.

The secret of Communication Mastery is taking charge of how you are perceived—known—not just by others but also to your Self.

One cornerstone of Spiritual Pragmatism is authenticity. The root of *authenticity* in part refers to "master/self/one who gains/authoritative." By the eighteenth century, authenticity came to mean "genuine." A fundamental key to unlocking our authentic Self is the Persona Statement. For decades, this has been one of the initial elements taught in the first session I have with every client.

I have had the privilege of teaching and working with one of the most significant business leaders in one of the highest profiled entertainment companies in the world. Peter is the chairman of this company, and he is personally and professionally of the highest integrity. He is a robust individual, confident and completely dedicated to what he does.

Although extremely successful for many years, he always had a desire to improve his public speaking abilities. When he first met me, we identified the multiple platforms we would concentrate on—media, board meetings, and public addresses were but a few on the list. I began by helping him craft his Persona Statement. He then chose the following key words to describe himself: *integrity, intelligence, passionate, honest, committed.* These words became a part of his brand. We went on to discuss that the Persona Statement is not designed to make you into somebody you are not, but bring out who you are capable of being. As previously stated in Chapter 1, we want the same person to show up everywhere.

With the Persona Statement as his template, Peter now had a key understanding of how to claim his authentic Self. Every public opportunity is calibrated in a way that remains true to the five key adjectives that were identified in his first Vocal Awareness lesson. From television interviews to press conferences, corporate events to keynote addresses, his Persona Statement informs everything he does. Peter's experience is a great example of how to be honest about what we ask of ourselves and how to integrate that integrity into everything we do through Communication Mastery.

Through the Mask

The Persona Statement is a way to remove our mask and reveal the Deeper Self in a more sovereign way.

The word *persona* in ancient Greece meant "mask," particularly one worn by an actor. It may have been borrowed from the Etruscan word *phersu*, "mask," which also meant "through the sound." In Vocal Awareness one's identity is "the sound of our voice coming through the mask." This notion of the mask helps us recognize that we all have guises, but the Persona Statement actually creates a profound opportunity for Self-discovery and Self-revelation.

As I developed the concept of Spiritual Pragmatism, I had to determine how the Persona Statement supports us in embodying our idealized version/vision of our Self in all contexts. When we speak of the Persona Statement, we are still speaking of *Conscious Awareness*. It is still about shifting behavior.

Through the Persona Statement we begin to learn to empower ourselves. We learn to *claim* who we are and be heard, not simply above but also through the din of daily discourse. Etymologically speaking, to *claim* means to *call out*. Our Persona Statement supports us in "calling ourselves out" every day. Acclaiming, exclaiming, proclaiming it in everything we are and actualizing it in everything we do. Everybody we meet in every walk of life projects a persona. More often than not, the projection is simply a collection of ideas, characteristics, and habits that have evolved over time. When crafting our Persona Statement for the first time, we are actually creating the opportunity to *choose* how we want to be known.

Our Persona Statement is the canvas on which we masterfully create the image of our authentic Self. As we learn to embody our Persona Statement, we are better able to confront our two greatest fears: abandonment and claiming our greatness.

Creating the Persona Statement

There are three steps to creating a Persona Statement. These steps focus on the recognition of both how we may currently be "perceived" and how we would prefer to be *known*.

Step 1. Take your time to honestly answer the following two questions.

Question 1: How do I believe I am presently perceived?

Consider the question from many perspectives. For example: friends, family, coworkers, strangers, acquaintances, and other important people/groups in your life. Simply write down what you feel their first impressions may be. For the moment you may use bullet points.

Question 2: How would I like to be perceived?

Keep in mind that this is your intrinsic identity, your truer inner Self—not just the self you show at work or in your social life. This is how you want to be known by everyone—all the time. Again, for the moment you may use bullet points.

Please reference the perceived perspectives you listed and distinguish between those you prefer, and those you do not. Include positive concepts only.

Step 2. Create visual representations of each of your two personas.

In addition to answering those two questions, please create two drawings to accompany your answers as outlined below. The drawings are important because they come from a deeper part of our unconscious.

Drawing 1: On a separate piece of paper, create a drawing that represents how you believe you are currently perceived.

Drawing 2: On a separate piece of paper, create a drawing that represents how you want to be perceived.

Don't worry about your talents as an artist. These representations are for your personal use. They can be stick figures, drawings, paintings, or different mediums such as clay or collage. Be open to color or black and white, abstract and/or realistic style, and as much simplicity or complexity as you feel you want. Allow your creative unconscious the freedom to play *without judgment*.

What do you observe about your two different images? Is one image more dramatic, colorful, or vibrant? Did something about your images surprise you?

Consider what you have discovered.

Step 3. You are now ready to write your Persona Statement.

Go back to the statement you wrote in answer to Question 2 and replace the phrase "I want to be perceived as . . ." with "I am." If you feel it is appropriate to change any of the other words, please do so.

All this work is metaphoric and, in the over four decades of my teaching, whether it be at a university, in the public or private sectors, or from whatever walk of life, this Persona Statement has become the template for beginning the transformative process. When we answer the second question, "How would I like to be perceived?" no longer answer it in bullet points such as "strong, successful, happy, fulfilled." Please write it in sentence form—for there is an important metaphor here. The metaphor is the period at the end of a thought. You are saying, "This is how I want to be known, *period*." You won't write any parenthetical caveat that says, "except when I'm lazy and I don't feel like it or when I'm anxious and I don't think I can." The period at the end of the sentence implies *all the time*.

There is also a second metaphor at work here: the fact that we actually have a choice in how we want to be known. As you have read, everything in life revolves around only two things—to choose or not to choose. It doesn't matter how scary it is, how seemingly daunting. All that matters is how badly you want it. This Work teaches Empowerment Through Voice. All we need to care about is, whether the choice made either empowers us or disempowers us? Choosing to write a Persona Statement and *choosing to* embody it will change your life. Embrace your transformation from being someone who may not have realized you had a choice into someone who knows life offers infinite possibilities.

Embodying the Persona Statement

After you have created the Persona Statement and assured yourself that this is how you want to be known, begin reading it out loud.

Once you are comfortable reading it aloud, please record yourself either in audio or on video as this will help you objectify a very intimate experience. Next, connect your Persona Statement to three or four sentences that reflect something you do professionally every day, or if you are in the job market, practice what you might say in your opening 15 seconds when speaking to a recruiter or potential employer. Each time you practice your statements, first be mindful of your Persona Statement. In these initial stages, you are developing your *Conscious Awareness*. These regular practice opportunities are critical. You are learning to put your Persona Statement into practice in the privacy of your personal space before walking out and embodying it in a public space.

Just a reminder that *we do not recognize how much work it takes to be our Selves in public*—how challenging it can be to simply *be* when someone else is watching. Little by little this practice regimen will help instill confidence, consistency, and familiarity. It will ultimately assure and reaffirm that who you have chosen to be is your birthright, that you no longer need to "ask permission" or to refrain from embodying in as integral a way as possible all of whom you are capable of Being—not just in a performance moment but in everything you do.

Next Steps

As you have begun to discover, Spiritual Pragmatism is a unique blend designed to integrate who we are into what we do. Life is a journey. To take any trip we need a very clear direction of where we are going and how we will get there. Now let's create a specific map for taking our journey.

The first step—visualize what you want. This is distinctly different than dreaming about what you want. In my first book in 1996, *The Sound of the Soul,* I created a character called the *pragmatic visionary*.

I stated that all the dreamer does is dream, but the pragmatic visionary dreams and then does what it takes to manifest that dream. This is an important distinction and one that often goes unnoticed. Remember, Communication Mastery is just that—mastery. Mastery always requires meticulous refinement and consistent attention to detail.

The second step—create an image of your vision. It can be a work of art that is a visual representation of your image, a drawing, a photograph, or a picture torn from a magazine. The point is this image must clearly represent your ultimate goal. For example, many of the athletes I have taught over the years have images in their journals and on the walls of their home that represent their goals and continuously inspire them to be their best and excel. For example, Emmitt Smith, who aspired to be the all-time leading rusher in the National Football League, had to overtake the former titleholder, Walter Payton. He maintained a portrait of this great athlete in his home office that motivated him. Perhaps yours is to be the chairman of a company and the visual is a chief executive, either male or female, running a board meeting.

One of my clients is the comptroller of her multinational corporation. Her goal is to be the CFO. The visual she and I have created is a montage of her company's logo, the executive office suite, and a photo of herself. Perhaps yours is to live a balanced life, have a comfortable home, a family and a job that is satisfying. What does that look like?

I've said for many years, "Not all of us aspire to pay the price to win an Academy Award, an Olympic gold medal, to have our own highly successful business, or to be the senior partner in a high-profile law firm." This exercise begins to help you focus on which price you *are* willing to pay. The point is, *everything costs something*, and we must be very clear about this. Too many of us live lives of regret and dissatisfaction—dreams unfulfilled, or jobs overtake our personal lives. One insight gleaned from this exercise is to discover what *you* want and to begin to manifest it to the best of your ability—*on your terms*. Now, begin to create your vision.

The third step—write out your Mission Statement. A Mission Statement is distinctly different from a goals statement, which will be discussed in step four. This statement is the contribution you want to make. On a personal note, excerpted here is a portion of my Mission Statement: "To change the world through Voice . . . To help all those I work with to achieve their own enlightenment and enjoy their own empowerment." My statement has evolved over many years and entails a deep reflection, among other things. Remember that you are creating a living document. As you invest in yourself and discover what it is you truly want, your Mission Statement will evolve until it becomes exactly what you want it to be. In the beginning, this process may be a bit unrefined. Many of my clients are even initially intimidated as they begin to put their thoughts on paper. Again, the two greatest fears—fear of abandonment and ownership of our power—raise their ignominious heads. Ultimately, these same clients persevere because as they learn in Vocal Awareness, the commitment is always to the Work. Perhaps it is helpful to begin your first Mission Statement with a list of words or phrases that reflect your values. Then you can shape them into sentences and paragraphs as you become clearer and more assured that this document is your Mission Statement.

The great use of a life is to spend it for something that outlasts it.
—William James

The fourth step is your Goals Statement. The Mission Statement is the contribution you want to make; the Goals Statement—with timeline—is how you will make your mission a reality.

We all have goals. These goals may include a part of our strategic plan as a business leader, our life goals, or even a personal New

Year's resolution. Although we all set goals, to be frank, often times they are not fulfilled. Perhaps we aim too high as we may have been unrealistic in identifying the resources needed and the time required for successful accomplishment. Another issue we have all confronted is sustaining our commitment to our stated goals when confronted with adversity of any sort. We become worn down, overwhelmed, intimidated, and turn away from our objective.

Please remember, the implicit goal of Vocal Awareness is Empowerment Through Voice. In this chapter, you are beginning to learn how to integrate your inner Voice through your outer voice. You are beginning to learn how to seamlessly embody your Self in full Conscious Awareness at all times. Spiritual Pragmatism helps us see what we previously never saw. Nowhere is this more critical than being able to define and fulfill our goals. Traditionally, we write our goals down and are satisfied. By doing so, we feel we have done what is necessary to accomplish what we set out to do. This is definitely not enough. Accountability and a clearly delineated plan are paramount in achieving our goals. Therefore, Vocal Awareness goals require a timeline. The framework for creating the most effective and efficient timeline is referred to in Vocal Awareness as 168 Hours.

168 Hours

There are 168 Hours in a week. This is finite. We have a choice as to how we spend our time, which creates an infinite number of possibilities during the 168 Hours. The 168 Hours exercise helps to identify how time is actually spent by keeping track of everything we do in a given week. Every day and every week is different, but the number of hours is consistent. Everything should be noted in the Vocal Awareness journal you have begun to create. Once you have identified how many hours you work on average, have calculated your sleep patterns, the time spent with family, and your commute time, you will have a baseline.

A number of years ago, my wife and I were having dinner in Malibu, California, with a theatrical client and his wife, who was from Madrid. During our meal she shared an axiom from her culture: "We work to live. In America you live to work." In the previous section, *Cost and Choice* were discussed, and the question of what price we are willing to pay was presented. One of the points of goal setting is identifying our answers to these questions—then, creating the plan. As previously stated, in this Work we learn to live life on our terms to the best of our ability. Based on this premise, I explained to my client's wife that, ideally, we do the Work that fulfills us personally and professionally. We live our lives and do our jobs in ways that honor us and fulfill the Vision we have for ourselves. In Vocal Awareness, the distinction between our work lives and our personal lives does matter, but what matters more is the integrative life. Her husband had been working with me for some time, and she was familiar with the Persona Statement which, as you now know, enables *the same person to show up everywhere*. The overarching goal is living a Consciously Aware life. This enables us to more effectively live life—period.

Matthew was a client of mine who became a close personal friend over our many years of working together. He was a lawyer, had his MBA, and had been a state controller. After retiring from his political career, he became a partner in a law firm. In our initial sessions, we began to make a game plan which, of course, included the creation of Vision, Mission, and Goals Statements. One of the first steps was to identify his goals. To help him do this, he embarked upon the168 Hours exercise. He traveled domestically and internationally, but managed to average the time he was in town. He found that he worked 102 hours per week. That left him only 66 hours per week to experience the rest of what he wanted to do in his life with his wife and two teenaged children, including sleep. With his newfound clarity, he created a practical and strategic system to live life more effectively. One of his new goals was to be a consultant for a global company. When he received an offer, a contract was negotiated that included an enhanced per diem and an extra first-class airline ticket that enabled him to take one of his children or his wife with him whenever he travelled. This is only one example of how the 168 Hours exercise can guide us in addressing not just our professional goals, but also our life goals in an integrative and effective way. In the beginnings of our relationship Matthew used to joke that when he passed away, it would be written on his tombstone that he was a hard worker who worked very long hours. He didn't know how prescient he was, for only eight years later, he did pass away—far too young. But, because of his trust of the Work and his commitment to his Self, the last part of his life was lived bountifully, conscientiously, and very much in balance.

Once again Communication Mastery is just that—mastery. As previously stated, mastery is in the subtlety. As we continue peeling back the layers of the onion, you are discovering the truth in the Vocal Awareness axiom, *Structure does not impinge, it liberates.* Instead of feeling *more vulnerable* as you reveal more, you are more empowered and confident. It is now time to introduce the final and crucial element in the narrative of Spiritual Pragmatism—The Hero's Journey.

The Hero's Journey:
The King's Speech

Many of us have heard the term and believe we understand the concept of The Hero's Journey. This is a phrase coined in 1949 by the leading mythologist of the twentieth century, Joseph Campbell. He taught at Sarah Lawrence College in Bronxville, New York, for

38 years. What Joseph Campbell created has meaningful and long-lasting value. We cannot successfully move forward in life as a people without remembering where we have been. One of the meaningful insights of Professor Campbell's work is consistently pointing out that stories found in all cultures are quite similar, whether in pre-Columbian cultures, African societies, American Indian folktales, or the Old Testament. In these powerful, mythical metaphors, we experience through projection of us into the character what it takes to vanquish our demons and overcome adversity by projecting ourselves into the characters. We learn through the mythical examples.

In Vocal Awareness, I interpret The Hero's Journey not as mythical, but as foundational to each and every one of our own personal experiences in our daily lives. We watch film, television and we see in one hour or 90 minutes conflict and resolution with commercials, but that is not real life. *Real life* is that an individual or team had an idea for a TV series or film many years before. They had to write that idea down. They had to develop that idea. They had to get support for their idea. They had to pitch the idea to producers, and studios, and likely were turned down time after time. For example, when Steven Spielberg was making the film *Jaws*, the production was almost shut down due to delays and budget overruns. Spielberg persisted, finished the film, and ultimately, it was an enormous success.

Simply stated, Steven Spielberg's persistence in taking an idea to fruition is an example of a heroic act. Realistically, most of us do not live life like this. We may have jobs in retail, real estate, health professions, and finance. Our jobs may be as assistants to executives, PBX operators, social workers, or teachers. We may be in business, but we may not be business leaders, and very important in today's challenging economy, we may even have trouble getting a job. In Vocal Awareness, the point of The Hero's Journey is factual, tactical, and pragmatic—what it takes to show up for ourselves and our families, day in and day out. How we confront adversity and not just overcome it, but vanquish it.

The Hero's Journey, helps us recognize as clearly as possible what it takes to live life to the best of our ability on our terms. *To fulfill our personal destiny is a heroic journey.* It is imperative that we see ourselves as our own heroes. In Vocal Awareness, The Hero's Journey is no longer mythology, but reality.

The King's Speech won an Academy Award in 2010 for Best Picture. It is a perfect example of what is necessary to take The Hero's Journey and live it, as well as deal with the consequences when taking the steps necessary to be his or her own hero.

The film was a touching portrait of the personal relationship between one of the twentieth century's first speech therapists, Lionel Logue, and King George VI of England who was a severe stutterer. Lionel Logue helped create The British Society of Speech Therapists in 1935.

In 1925, when King George VI was the Duke of Windsor and not yet crowned King of England, he succeeded his elder brother in a presentation at the Empire Exhibition in Wembley, England. The previous year thousands of people had watched the slim figure of his elder brother do an elegant job opening the exhibition. The 1924 exhibition was the first time his father's, King George V, and his brother's voices were captured on live broadcast by the British Broadcasting Corporation. King George V even noted in his diary: "Everything went off most successfully."[2]

The speech the Duke was to present was brief, and he had practiced the delivery numerous times, but his sheer dread of public speaking created a stultifying, terrifying personal experience for him. He felt so hopeless that even when he spoke in front of his father, he would become increasingly nervous over the simplest effort. Writing to his father, he said "I shall be very frightened as you have never heard me speak and the loud speakers are apt to put off one as well."[3]

When the moment finally arrived, the Duke's actual speech was broadcast not only in the British Isles, but around the world. To summarize the presentation in one word, it was humiliating. There were even moments when he attempted to speak and no sound came out of his mouth. It was simply sheer determination that enabled him to get through it.

The Duke was second in line to the throne, yet he conspicuously had failed at one of his most important tasks—effectively delivering a public speech. What had previously been known only in private and family circles instantly became public knowledge—not simply in Great Britain but around the world.

The following year the, Duke of Windsor, was introduced to Lionel Logue and the Work began. During their first meeting in October 1926, Logue was able to help him trace his impediment back to his childhood. "I can hear *you*," Logue declared at the end of this session which lasted an hour and a half, "but it will need a tremendous effort by you. Without that effort, it can't be done."[4]

They worked consistently for the next 14 months. What ultimately helped the Duke overcome something he previously thought impossible to overcome was the unique teaching regimen that Logue created for him and the extraordinary effort the Duke, the future King, put into his daily exercise. "Every spare moment he had outside his official duty was spent on practicing and doing exercises."[5] If he was out hunting, he made sure he came back early to put in an hour's work with Logue before dinner. If he was on an official engagement, he would arrange for a break to allow him to fit in his lesson. All of that dedicated effort began to pay off within the first several months and, with each breakthrough, he was compelled to work even harder. From the beginning of their journey together, there was implicit trust, dedication, and hard work from teacher to student and reciprocated from student to teacher. They had formed a partnership.

Partnership is critical in all transformational work, but never more so than it is in the intricate partnership required in Vocal Awareness. This partnership is not only between teacher and student; it begins with the partnership with your Self.

In Communication Mastery it is imperative you understand the importance of trust and commitment to the Work—of not just *doing* the exercises but focusing on the *quality of how* we do our exercises. This insightful story is about the relationship of these two men from completely different walks of life—one an aristocrat, the other a gentleman from Australia. They came together to create something more than they could have created by themselves. This is a clear example of the importance of partnership and of "answering the Call." What we are called to do and how we are called to serve is what matters. When we know we are called, we can't simply say "wrong number," and hang up.

Lionel Logue appeared in the future King's life at one of the most significant moments of the twentieth century. They met in 1926 and when King George V passed, the Duke's brother abdicated. Nine years after that meeting, with the world on the brink of war, the Duke became King George VI. Three years later war between England and Germany was declared.

Time and money spent in improving the voice pay a larger interest than any other investment.

—William Gladstone[6]

Almost 11 years after his first meeting with Logue, King George VI was to have a public coronation in Westminster Abbey. As the day approached, the King became increasingly nervous. In preparation for the coronation, the King met again with Logue. The cordiality and trust of their partnership immediately resumed, and they began working on the King's coronation speech. As the

King prepared for the coronation, things didn't always go smoothly. Disturbing comments from behind-the-scenes were made by some members of the King's retinue about the King's "impediment" or even suggestions that the King find someone other than Logue to help him.

On the sixth day of practice, the rehearsal went very badly, and the King went into a rage, but his wife was able to calm him. The next day the rehearsal was recorded by the BBC. It was "too slow and the King was disgusted with it. They tried again, but halfway through he wanted to cough so they had to make yet another attempt."[7]

Whether in the world of broadcasting or a simple public statement, everyone has an opinion about public discourse. These opinions may not always be informed—they are just that, opinions. However, we do tend to listen to them. We are completely exposed when publicly revealing something that has been kept private. Again, as a point of emphasis, *we do not realize how much work it takes to be ourselves in public—while others watch.*

One of the reasons I've chosen to include The Hero's Journey with the poignant story of *The King's Speech* in this section is because, whether it be the world stage or a corporate stage, at some level, our presentation is trial by fire. *If we are not there for ourselves, no one will be there for us.* If we do not do what is required of us, no matter what it takes, we cannot fulfill our destiny. This can affect not only us, but the corporation or, in this case, the nation and, ultimately, the world.

The King and Logue listened to a recording the King had made earlier—five days before the coronation. They both agreed it would be good enough to be broadcast. They also hoped it would not be necessary.

Quoting from Logue's diary: "H. M. improves every day, getting good control of his nerves and his voice, is getting some wonderful tones into it. . . . He is such a good chap—and I do want him to be a marvelous King."[8]

This sweet reflection is a reminder of the importance of the Vocal Awareness principle of *surrender*—to yield or to give back. In other words, to be in service. Lionel Logue had a stunning insight when he recognized that it was not only his role as teacher but also what he did in his role that helped the King fulfill his responsibility as monarch. This is paradoxical: *To be there for the Work, we have to be there for our Selves. When we are there for our Selves, we are there for the Work.*

The King's speech was a triumph. Quoting from *The Daily Mail*: "At the sound of the King's voice and the purity of his diction . . . with all the depth of his father's voice, there is an additional softness which makes it even more impressive to the listener."[9] *The Detroit Free Press* radio noted that night: ". . . what became of the speech impediment that King George VI was supposed to have? It wasn't apparent throughout the entire ceremony and, after hearing the new King deliver his address, many persons are classifying him with President Roosevelt as possessing a perfect radio voice."[10]

Three years later, war broke out and, along with Winston Churchill, King George VI helped inspire his nation through the power of his voice via radio. The observation from *The Daily Mail* about the tone of his voice is a reminder that it is not just about *what we say*, but *how we say it*. One of the undercurrents of this book and one of the key streams of thought coursing throughout is the energy—the vibration—of our intrinsic sound. These opportunities are usually squandered during daily discourse simply because we are unaware.

The life of King George VI and what it took for him to *be his best* is a compelling example of what happens when we surrender to the Deeper Self and to our commitment to the Work.

You will recall the Vocal Awareness axiom that everything revolves around two things: to choose or not to choose—and, even in abdication, one clearly makes a choice. The only consideration is: Does our choice empower us or disempower us? Nowhere is this choice more profoundly important than when we choose to embark on our own Hero's Journey.

Please do not misconstrue that our journey is only about when we may be called to greatness. That is not at all the point—in fact, that may be the excuse. If we are not called to greatness, what heroic journey do we have to take? The very point is that The Hero's Journey is not just for ennobled moments in our lives such as preparing to deliver a stellar keynote address, chair a shareholders' meeting, or run for President of the United States. It is always about our *journey*—not only about when we arrive at key moments on that journey. A successful job interview is a heroic act. Steeling your courage and confidently asking for a raise is a heroic act.

When Lionel Logue and the future King George VI met, there was no way to determine where their working relationship would take them almost a decade later. They were not only concerned with the outcome, they were sharing the journey. As you set your course, it is essential to have a global view in mind, but equally essential to do what it takes each and every step of the way. This is how to achieve personal sovereignty, which is a necessary requisite for each of us to fulfill our heroic possibility.

Action Step ··········➤

In your communication journal, design your Persona, Vision, Mission, and Goals Statements. Please begin to strategize how you spend your 168 Hours. Reflect upon your Hero's Journey.

4

THE VOCAL AWARENESS METHOD: MASTERING THE JOURNEY

Nothing in the world can take the place of persistence. Talent will not; nothing is more common than unsuccessful men with talent. Genius will not; unrewarded genius is almost a proverb. Education will not; the world is full of educated derelicts. Persistence and determination alone are omnipotent.

—President Calvin Coolidge

The Power of Practice

Every day we experience each other's lives as we observe one another speak, walk, gesture—live. Through this lens, we *read* joy, strength, fear, anxiety, and so much more. We then use these subtle observations to either include or marginalize ourselves and/or others. For example, when we approach a business meeting with fear and trepidation, our colleagues lose confidence in us. Equally important, these events cause us to doubt ourselves. As you have read, we behave in our habituated ways for so long and for so many reasons that we no longer recognize this behavior and/or know we can do it differently.

Through the Vocal Awareness principles you have begun to incorporate, such as your Persona Statement and Spiritual Pragmatism, you now understand that this Work is a systematic approach to achieving Life Mastery. Integral to this process are the concepts you are about to learn—Stature and the 7 Rituals. Including Stature and the 7 Rituals into your life puts you in the driver's seat on the road to your own destiny. These Rituals are often referred to as The Checklist. By adding The Checklist to your process, you will experience an added dimension in your communication and will be better able to control the course of all encounters—professional or personal. This is true Life and Communication Mastery.

To gain the maximum benefits of Vocal Awareness, you will create a Daily Practice that can be accomplished in 7 minutes a day. The payoff for this Practice is extraordinary—you gain Conscious Awareness and the ability to live with greater meaning and purpose.

The 7 Rituals, in conjunction with your Persona Statement and consistently embodying yourself in Stature, are foundational to your strategy for success. This structure will prepare you for every situation from the mundane to the most significant and enable you to consistently Claim Your Voice and Claim Your Power.

I began working with the Ritz-Carlton Hotel Company in 1984 during the preopening of the Laguna Niguel, California, property. The company had begun to institute what they call the "Ritz-Carlton Basics." I began to train the employees, beginning with the food and beverage director, then on to the bellmen, PBX and the executive team. The Vocal Awareness "basics"—the Persona Statement, Stature, and 7 Rituals—were incorporated into every session. For example, in support of their motto, "We are ladies and gentlemen serving ladies and gentlemen," all staff members learned how to embody this motto as themselves in full Conscious Awareness in a seamlessly natural way from the way they spoke with one another and the guests to the way they walked. In addition, every element of the Ritz-Carlton Basics was interpreted through Vocal Awareness. The employees learned the same techniques and principles being taught in this chapter.

As you undertake the work of this chapter and begin to acquire the requisite skills to support your Communication Mastery, please stop each step of the way and experience the subtle and not so subtle distinctions of this Work. I don't want you to simply *go through the motions,* I would rather you stop and, as discerningly as possible, experience each step of the journey. You are developing Conscious Awareness, learning to be more attuned to everything. This is a course in mastery. *All* of the elements matter. Learn them and practice them linearly, which will enable you to embody them integratively. Ultimately, there are two key understandings in any discipline for mastery to be achieved. First, mastery requires integration of mind/body/spirit. Second, it involves mastering the subtleties of form. Speaking with a former Wimbledon champion, I drew parallels between the mastery she knew as a great tennis player and the mastery of this Work. I rhetorically asked, "How many thousands of hours did you practice tossing the ball in the air and establishing the exact moment to make contact on your serve, your footwork, follow through, baseline shots, backhand, eye/hand coordination—everything! Also, it wasn't just the mechanics of the game you practiced, but equally important, your internal calibration—focus, courage, confidence, commitment, and so forth. Vocal Awareness is teaching you how to refine a new skill, public speaking. However, the principles of mastery are the same—ritual and attention to detail repeated over and over again until they define who you are. Please always remember, *A Champion Does It Differently!* It is never merely the reps; it is the quality of the reps."

Stature

We have heard the term "stature" before. Before Vocal Awareness, it had been used to describe our literal height, or even our place in society. How well regarded we are among our peers is an example of the original description. In Vocal Awareness, Stature means something very different: *Stature is the preparation for everything we do and the embodiment of all we are.*

When you physically assume good posture, you might feel stronger and superficially appear more confident. But, notice something as you sit or stand with good posture or at attention. Taking a mental inventory, you may notice you are holding your breath, holding tension in your tongue, jaw, neck, or shoulders. You may feel less than *natural*, perhaps even subtly guarded or presentational. In contrast, Stature is not only a physical expression, it is also a *state of mind*, as well as a *state of being*. It lifts you physically, emotionally, and spiritually.

Everything in Vocal Awareness is connected physiologically. There is nothing in this Work that is *only* mental, emotional, psychological, or spiritual. Our intellectual learning may be linear, but the body's experience is integrative. For example, as you put yourself in Stature, feel an imaginary thread pulling from the top of your head, extending you, lifting your abdominal muscles. The physical impulse for all this—and the first thing the body does when you access Stature—is to breathe. Please stop and notice this physical impulse.

The more we inhabit *Stature*, the more we consciously recognize and subsequently eliminate any physical slump we may have habitually adopted as the way to interface with the world. In addition not only do we eliminate a physical slump, which changes our outward appearance, but Stature also enhances our physical energy as the body is better aligned. Thus, it becomes physiologically more efficient.

Stature is not a ritual, it is preparation for everything we do. In Vocal Awareness, always begin your practice in front of a mirror. This may be difficult for any number of reasons. It may require consummate discipline. But the root of the word *discipline* does not mean "cracking the whip," it means "teaching" *or* "learning." In this regard, your practice need never be harsh or judgmental, but rather conscientious and patient. The mirror helps objectify—enabling us to see what others see. This is critical in correcting negative behaviors. *Remember: mastery is in the subtlety.* As you begin to learn, you begin to teach yourself. As in all learning, *self-correction is paramount.* Engaging Stature may feel forced or unnatural. However, as you observe yourself in the mirror and self-correct at all times, you will see that you look better and appear more authentic. As you gain confidence living in Stature, you will be breaking lifelong habits that may have held you down and back for a very long time.

Many years ago I taught the noted motivational speaker Tony Robbins. Tony referred to Stature and the 7 Rituals as "pattern interrupts." He said, "To break any habit, one has to exaggerate a new behavior to break that habit." Dancers in preparation for their performance may stand in first position. One cannot *sort of* stand in first position. There is only one way to do it. One cannot *sort of* break habits, or *sort of* stand in Stature or do any of this Work. Please be Consciously Aware and consistent as you acquire your new skills. There is an important Vocal Awareness axiom that is relevant here: *Caution creates anxiety—conscientiousness creates awareness.*

The meeting begins before you walk into the room. As the dancer walks onto the stage in character and stands in first position, the baseball player stands in the on-deck circle preparing for his at-bat, in business/life Stature becomes your first position—your on-deck circle moment in everything you do and everywhere you go.

7 Rituals: The Checklist

In fall 2011, I did a public seminar for business leaders in Amsterdam. The following day, I concluded a similar seminar at the Rotterdam School of Management. A psychologist from Brussels was one of the people in attendance. Two weeks after the seminar, I received an e-mail from him that I paraphrase here:

> *I've been practicing the 7 Rituals regularly. I pay a lot of attention to Stature. All of my life people have told me that I walk funny.. Also, my wife often reminds me that I should try to walk more upright, but it has always been difficult for me to do so. Additionally, I've had a lot of pain in my shoulder muscle and only a massage or stretching helped temporarily. However, since practicing the Stature exercise, the pain is almost gone. It seemed that the pain was caused by a wrong Stature. Sometimes things are so simple. . . . Another thing that is really working for me is the 5th Ritual—Take My Time. I'm paying much more attention when I speak, and I'm taking my time to choose my words. Something really interesting happened recently. I'm Belgian, but I grew up in Germany the first 20 years of my life. For the last 20 years, I've been living in Brussels and I have little possibility to speak German. I do read German books and watch German television sometimes, but I avoid speaking the language because it is as if my brain can't find the right German words. Last week, however, I had a phone call with an old friend in German. The conversation was very fluent, and I realized that it was so fluent because I was much more aware when I spoke. It felt as if my brain had more time to find the right words because I slowed down a bit when I spoke . . .*

As you know, Communication Mastery requires two imperatives: mastering the subtlety of form—mastery is never simplistic or unconscious—and understanding that all mastery requires the integration of mind/body/spirit. Whether it is the athlete's pregame rituals, or the artist in the wings preparing to come on stage, that moment of physical or mental preparation is never only biomechanical—it is also spiritual.

Also, please notice the phrase mind/body/spirit is written with slash lines, not with commas or the word and. The reason for this is because, once again, in this Work, it is implicit we understand *everything is always integrative*. Even when the words are sequential as they are here, the slash line visually denotes the gestalt of mastery—the wholeness.

I recognize that it is not traditional or conventional to speak about rituals or spirituality in a business context. But, as Communication Mastery establishes a new paradigm, "at the beginning and end of the day," it unabashedly teaches Self Mastery. When I codified the following Rituals over 40 years ago, they were designed to help us be our very best. As you discovered in the last chapter, there is no distinction about where to be our very best. Business/life is one and the same. The Checklist is the foundation for everything you will do going forward. You will learn to employ it before every presentation. You will also notice it spontaneously coming to mind while you speak extemporaneously, and it will never intrude—it will always be welcomed.

As you begin this part of the journey, please do not overthink things. You do not need empirical evidence or intellectual understanding for the principles to be effective. In this context, a Vocal Awareness axiom comes to mind: employ the KISS approach—Keep It Simple, Sweetheart. Initially, I suggest you read through the 7 Rituals. It is acceptable to explore them intellectually for a moment. For now, a basic familiarity with the language and the concepts is all that is needed. Following the written explanation of the 7 Rituals, the daily Vocal Awareness Workout and a practice protocol called The Three Aspects will be presented. In the next section called Learning the Fundamentals, you will be instructed step-by-step in how to do the Work. The written text and explanation will be supported with meticulous images so you can clearly see how to do the Work.

Let's begin!

Ritual 1: Thank You to My Source.

What *Thanking Source* means depends on our belief system. At this time, the only understanding necessary is that Thanking Source represents the profound moment when we both surrender and connect to the infinite, to something outside of our mere physical reality.

Everything begins with and is connected to Source. Everything flows through Source. Vibrationally and energetically, Source is the reservoir from which all things originate. Whether we are conscious of it or not, Source is the foundational principle integrating mind/body/spirit.

When we acknowledge Source, the first thing our bodies do is inhale. Notice I don't say, "We take a breath," as this is not a conscious act, and that is the point. When we say "thank you," the body intuits its appreciation by inhaling deeply. This instinctive breath is the body's way of saying, "Thank you for giving me permission to be me," and breathes in acknowledgment.

In our minds, as we *consciously* repeat Ritual 1: "Thank You to My Source," a transformative change actually occurs. We no longer fear that which we had previously feared the most—Claiming Our Power and Embodying Our Greatness. In this empowered state, all things are possible.

Ritual 2: Love and Let Go.

One of the more subtle but important distinctions in Vocal Awareness is recognition that "we don't know what we don't know."

Ritual 2 is critical in helping us confront, shed light on, and supportively deal with any aspect of our lives that heretofore we may have been afraid to acknowledge or that may have been hidden from us. The insights and clarity that emerge as a result of this ritual also give us access to fulfilling possibilities we didn't know existed.

Generally, we are not used to the idea that we can *actually* be all that we conceive. This recognition may sometimes frighten or intimidate us. This trepidation often causes us to be *the cork in our own bottle.*

In Ritual 1, the body inhales as it surrenders to Source. In this moment our mind/body/spirit connection is fearless as we experience emotional and spiritual support. In Ritual 2, the body's first impulse is also to inhale. This response recognizes our intrinsic right to own our power for which we also have to take responsibility. In the first act we surrender; in the second act we reclaim our *intrinsic right to be ourselves.* We can achieve what we may only have dreamed of. Every time we engage these rituals, we energetically reprogram ourselves—we create a disciplined accountability that enables us to return to the integrity of our vision and take action.

Ritual 3: Allow a Slow, Silent, Conscious, Loving Breath.

Breath is fuel. If we don't put gas in our cars, we will not get to our destination. By the same token, if we do not breathe effectively, we cannot speak effectively. This critical pattern interrupt introduces us to the recognition that breath is not only physical, but also emotional and spiritual. The root of the word *spirit—spiritus*—means to breathe. When practicing Ritual 3 in an exercise context, your inhalation takes five to six seconds. It is never rushed or forced and is always silent. Initially, it doesn't matter whether you breathe through your nose or your mouth. This specific note is another subtle distinction in Vocal Awareness. Rushing and then presenting creates untold tension in yourself and in your listener. By retraining your breathing patterns, you are shifting behavior from rushing and presenting to a redefined focus where you gain control and are better able to be in Communication Mastery.

When we allow a *Slow, Silent, Conscious, Loving Breath*, we deliberately shift our unconscious habits away from paying little or no attention to what we are doing to *always* being Consciously Aware. In this way, we become better integrated and connected to our mind/body/spirit. Remember, the goal is always embodiment—whether in performance, on the telephone, over coffee, with our families, during a presentation—in every aspect of life. In Vocal Awareness/Communication Mastery, we use breath to both connect us and to open us to ourselves and others.

Ritual 4: See the Edge and Arc of Sound.

To See the Edge and Arc of Sound requires complete sensory integration—visual, auditory, and vocal. It is based in part on the Bernoulli Effect which states that, as the speed of a gas or liquid increases, the pressure it exerts upon its surrounding environment decreases. Thus, as a plane moves forward, the air that passes over its wings exerts

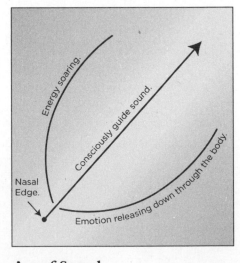

Arc of Sound

less pressure, allowing the plane to lift. Our breath also lifts and soars as it leaves our bodies. When we focus on this lift by following through *visually* and energetically, we experience more power, more emotion, and ultimately more communication freedom and confidence. To understand Ritual 4, we have to first experience it. In this case intellectual understanding doesn't help us.

> **Vocal Awareness is a *being work*, but *we always have to do to be.***

Ritual 4 consists of two distinct parts that are integrally connected: the Edge and the Arc. The Edge is your visual point of focus. You discover it by placing your fingernail—please note, not your fingertip—on the very edge of the center of your top lip, your lip line. It is your "sweet spot" akin to hitting the dot on your golf ball or striking a tennis ball at the center of the racket. It is the exact point at which you mentally focus your attention every time you warm up your voice or speak, and it is critical to your success in Communication Mastery.

After the sound leaves your body, your focus becomes the Arc. Sound doesn't leave your mouth or travel to a fixed point and then stop, it continues energetically *through* space. Athletes run or throw *through* a target, they don't run or throw *at* a target. When you *know* this and *consciously* follow through with your sound, this concept will help you speak *through the end* of your thought, not *to the end* of your thought. This will help you maintain a more consistent voice and create a dynamic delivery. Please note an arc is not an arch. In Vocal Awareness, you are training your voice to sustain energy and soar, which will also help release added emotion and expression.

Vocal Awareness exercises will be introduced following the 7 Rituals.

Ritual 5: Take My Time.

The fact is each of us has a finite amount of time in which to communicate. This is true in business meetings, public addresses, job interviews, or the proverbial elevator pitch. Some may think this means we need to speak quickly and say as much as we can in the time allotted. But, in fact, what is most important is not how fast we speak, but how effectively we communicate. Nothing is gained by going too fast. However, everything could be lost. You could lose the attention of your listener or audience, create misunderstandings in what you are trying to convey, or even make mistakes in your delivery or content that may go unnoticed.

As you discover the strategic importance of taking your time in Ritual 5, everything in your daily life and professional encounters will change. It will be easier to notice if you are rushing, bustling, or appearing anxious as you walk or speak. You will recognize that these behaviors directly impact how others perceive you (remember everything you do and say must reflect your Persona Statement—your Brand). Also, as illustrated in the earlier example from the psychologist in Belgium, when you slow down, you gain tactical *thinking time*. You will discern an immediate shift in even the most basic conversation as you *gain control not just of the message, but the messenger.* Being in charge to the best of your ability is always the goal.

Ritual 6: Pay Attention/Deeper Listening.

Throughout this book, you have noticed the word "voice" written both with an uppercase "V" and a lowercase "v." The reason for this distinction is Ritual 6. The lowercase "v"—voice—refers to the spoken word, which is our *outer voice*. The capital "V"—Voice—

refers to the *inner voice*. In Vocal Awareness, this is known as the Deeper Self. This is the core of who you are capable of being—not merely how you behave. This Ritual establishes the opportunity in a consistent and disciplined way to observe how you communicate at all times. Through Ritual 6 you learn how to "pay attention" on the outside while "listening deeply" on the inside to the voice and message only you hear. This technique enables us to be bolder and more authentic. We learn not only to speak or hear on the outside as we always have, but also to listen to what we know to be true on the inside and simultaneously stay connected to that. What emerges is a conscious confidence—a state of *being* who you are rather than presenting who you are. This ability is fundamental to personal mastery and integral to Communication Mastery. Your Voice *is* your identity. The embodiment of Ritual 6 helps put all the elements of Vocal Awareness together and leads directly into the final ritual, "Be My Self."

Ritual 7: Be My Self.

Consistently and consciously give your Self permission to *be who you are and never present who you are*. When exposed to the three words "Be My Self," most will see the same ubiquitous two words: Be myself—lowercase, "myself," as this is the usual way of writing this phrase. Then, as "myself" is separated into two words, please notice how you better understand the depth and clarity of the word "Self." "Self" equates to the Deeper Self. The Deeper Self is the impeccable, intimate, intrinsic aspect available to each of us.

Through Stature and the 6 Rituals, the goal is to attain the ability to live in the 7th—Be My Self. As you engage Ritual 7 each day in full Conscious Awareness, you set foot on your path—at work, at home, and at play—in a forthright and dedicated way. Through Ritual 7 you enhance and claim your authentic Self in all ways and at all times. To *Be My Self* is to embody the synergistic blend of mind/body/spirit in complete Conscious Awareness. This is both intrapersonal and interpersonal Communication Mastery.

The Daily Vocal Awareness Workout

First, to put your daily Vocal Awareness Workout in context, to be in Communication Mastery requires maximum vocal development. Every athlete, dancer, or singer I have ever trained or known prepares their body or their instrument for every competition or every performance. How many of you in your daily lives do the same for your voice? If not, why not? You are a professional. You make your living with your voice and your mind as they do. It is only logical that you would do what it takes to be at your optimal best. But, until you read these words, it may not have occurred to you that training your voice is not only prudent but necessary. Athletes spend a significant amount of time each day stretching their hamstrings, the longest muscles in the body. Look at the complete disregard we show for our larynx, the smallest muscle in the body. Athletes, dancers, and singers function in highly competitive environments. They are well trained and prepared for every encounter.

Is it any different for you in the business world? Of course not. Each artist and athlete, more or less, does the same drills. As you incorporate the Vocal Awareness Workout in your daily plan, you will have to sustain it in a vacuum. No one else will be doing the Work with you. You *must* sustain it by yourself. This is a critical point. The investment of time and energy you are making is for your Self. What I am asking you to take stock of at this moment is that in Communication Mastery, it is equally important to maximize every performance opportunity and to prepare your vocal muscles and your body to be ready to perform at your maximum best at all times. It is a normal routine to stretch our bodies when we exercise at the gym, go jogging, and the like. The Vocal Awareness Workout that you are being introduced to will become your *new normal* and the benefits will be immediately discernible.

Several years ago I was voted "The Best of the Best" as a YPO resource. YPO is an acronym for Young Presidents Organization— an international consortium of significant global business leaders. The following exercises you are about to learn are always a part of each event, regardless of whether I'm speaking in Las Vegas, Nevada, or Edinburgh, Scotland. There are two reasons I include them in this presentation. *One, they are fundamental to the integrity of Communication Mastery, and two, they are the missing piece in all leadership development work.* Each executive who attends YPO conferences does so in part because they know they will always discover something new they did not know. The new discoveries will enhance who they are and/or what they do. The Vocal Awareness Workout does just that. It gives them the personal insight and communication edge they have been seeking.

As you do the following exercises, please do not approach them as calisthenics. Yes, it is a Vocal Awareness Workout, but it is art as well. Approach them as a dancer would stretch at the barre—elegantly, intently, and artistically. An appropriate analogy is comparing a world-class gymnast with a Cirque du Soleil performer. They are both gymnasts. An Olympic gymnast does amazing things in the sport. What the Cirque du Soleil performer does is astonishing and equally incomprehensible, but you don't see the effort, you only see the art. Their goals are different—one is athleticism, the other is performance art.

The Vocal Awareness Workout is designed to enable you to vocally and presentationally express your Persona, Vision/Mission, and Goals Statements at all times—to do so is equally exceptional. Frankly, you cannot *be* your best without them. It may take time to emotionally adjust so you don't feel awkward, silly, or judgmental.

If you need support, use your Checklist. *The Checklist is always your due north.* It may also be challenging to find a place to practice. If you practice at home, explain to your family the types of exercises you are going to be doing. You will discover if there is any emotional discomfort that lies within you. As you get over the hump, you will be able to do these exercises virtually everywhere. I don't expect you to be as cavalier as I—for I have done them almost any place you can imagine. I figure I am never going to see these people again, so it really doesn't matter what they think of me vocalizing. I have practiced in the shower, public men's rooms, hotel rooms, airplanes, and even walking down the street. Every single one of my clients has done their Vocal Awareness Workout before each public event, whether it was a Wall Street Quarterly Report, a shareholders' meeting, a critical teleconference, an interview, or a broadcast. As they need to be at their best, their commitment begins with the following exercises. Enjoy the discoveries that await you!

So far, you have gained a basic understanding of the Vocal Awareness Method and some of the communication challenges it will resolve. We have discussed how each of us is an integrated mind/body/spirit system and explored fundamental principles including Stature and the 7 Empowerment Rituals, a.k.a. the Vocal Awareness Checklist. You will now learn a series of basic exercises using sound and breath. This will then be followed by a 7-minute daily practice routine and success tips. Please remember *the routine is never routine.* Each time you do an exercise, integrate the Checklist principles.

During your first few sessions, while you are learning how to do these techniques effectively, deliberately, and conscientiously, take time to stop and reflect on the physical sensations you feel as well as your emotions and attitude. You will come to discover that is a good life strategy too. Soon, the logic and elegance of the program will become apparent. The Vocal Awareness Method is more than a theory—it is a direct experience. *You actually need to do it to understand it.*

Once you have learned the basic Vocal Awareness Workout, please practice it in the morning every day. If you do not, you will discover it is much more difficult to do it later in the day or in the evening, as there is a chance you may never get to it. I call this "teeth brushing." You don't leave home without brushing your teeth; please don't leave home without doing Vocal Awareness. You are forming a new behavior that requires discipline and a strong commitment. This process is not unlike going on a diet. One reason weight loss centers are such profitable businesses is that most of us lose and gain back the same 10 pounds over and over again. To lose weight, we actually have to stick to the plan. Commit to doing the Vocal Awareness Workout daily a minimum of 7 minutes for 7 days. Then, renew your commitment for another week, then another, and so on.

As your Vocal Awareness Workout becomes an ingrained behavior, you can decide whether it fits better somewhere else in your daily schedule. When not traveling for business, I get up at 3:00 a.m. or 3:30 a.m. to pray and meditate. This solitudinal time is imperative. I then go to the gym followed by an hour walk with my wife. Next is additional Vocal Awareness time. If I'm on the road or there is a late night, my Ritual time begins later but always precedes the rest of my day. As stated before, *Structure does not impinge, it liberates.*

The craft you will develop in your daily Vocal Awareness Workout can also be used immediately prior to "performance" situations, such as important meetings, job interviews, critical conference calls, sales calls, and on-air appearances—all public presentations. You will discover these techniques to be invaluable as you shift and anchor your focus in as little as a minute, 30 seconds, or literally in a single breath. Make a detour to the restroom for a few moments if there's nowhere else to go to get some privacy. Ultimately you can even derive significant benefit when engaging in the Work silently— *seeing* the Rituals and their interface in the ensuing presentation in your mind's eye. The more often you consciously prepare your voice with these warm-up techniques, the more deeply ingrained Communication Mastery becomes.

Preparing for a Vocal Workout: Gathering Tools

For the purpose of hygiene, please wash your hands before you begin. You will be placing your hands on your face and, eventually, your fingers under your tongue. In addition, you will need:

➤ A mirror to observe yourself.

➤ A washcloth or handkerchief necessary for the Tongue Pull exercise.

➤ A pencil or Bic-type pen to help with a more advanced technique.

➤ A recording device (audio or video), which will help you gain objective feedback.

➤ The Vocal Awareness Rituals—The Checklist.

➤ Your Persona Statement—it is imperative to consistently interface with it until it is "naturally" a part of your communication DNA.

➤ Your Vocal Awareness journal to record your observations and impressions.

For some, recording your workouts may be stressful or even seem impossible to do. However, please persevere. Be steadfast and strive to approach every feedback session in an objective and non-judgmental fashion. It is your opportunity to learn and grow in a way you have never experienced before. It is incumbent upon you to establish a respectful and safe space, internally and externally, in which to do the Work. In the beginning it is easy to be thwarted and give up—remember the two greatest fears. Doing your daily Vocal Awareness Workout establishes protocols that ultimately enable you *to own your voice and own your power.*

The Vocal Workout Exercises: The Three Aspects

The Three Aspects are the framework of your Vocal Awareness Workout. Use them as your preparation for every performance. I define a "performance" as any situation where you need to be at your best whether it be a routine activity that you formerly took for granted or a keynote address.

> ➤ **The First Aspect—The Warm-Up.** During the Warm-Up, 90 percent of your focus will be on your technique—that is, your mind/body/spirit awareness—and 10 percent on aesthetics, or the quality of your voice. The First Aspect is where the discovery and attunement begin as you stretch your vocal muscles and warm up your voice. Each time you warm up is an opportunity to calibrate your inner Voice/outer voice with your Persona Statement. Please remember you are creating alignment and Conscious Awareness. The First Aspect is the first step you take each day on the road to full Communication Mastery and Empowerment Through Voice.

> ➤ **The Second Aspect—The Bridge.** The Bridge is a transition between the warm-up and the actual performance. During the Second Aspect, 65 percent of your fo-

cus will be on your technique and 35 percent on aesthetic quality. You will now apply the technical aspects of Vocal Awareness to the words you are preparing to speak. This could be a prepared speech, bullets for an extemporaneous conversation, PowerPoint text, and so on.

➤ **The Third Aspect—The Performance.** Your focus has now come full circle—10 percent of your attention is on "mechanics" and 90 percent is on the quality of delivery. Your style, the sound of your voice, body language, tempo, cadence, and pitch—everything is integrated each and every time in Conscious Awareness.

The Three Aspects are an exceedingly valuable matrix for achieving Communication Mastery. The meticulous attention to detail and consistent deconstruction and reassembling of *what you say and how you say it* is identical to what has been done throughout the millennia in all forms of mastery.

Learning the Fundamentals

There are many reasons for doing the following exercises, some of which have already been discussed. What hasn't been explicitly addressed is the act of gaining access through these exercises to your Voice. For example, as you release tension in your jaw, tongue, neck, and shoulders, your voice is freer and has more amplitude—enhanced vocal color. Your face and eyes appear more expressive, your mouth more relaxed. Therefore, you are perceived as less stressed or anxious and, by extension, subliminally recognized as more confident and a stronger leader. In addition, your body language and body image are more relaxed and congruent and better reflect your idealized persona. Equally important, of course, is the fact that each time you do these exercises, you are discarding old habits and embedding new ones. This strategic incremental approach is requisite in your ongoing commitment to being your best.

Just as you need a solid foundation to erect a strong building, you likewise need a solid foundation to build a strong Voice. It is important to take your time and learn how to do the exercises properly and effectively. The structure of the techniques and the daily Vocal Awareness Workout that builds upon them is very specific—you must adhere to the guidelines in order to reap the maximum benefit. It is likely to take several sessions to integrate all the instruction you're about to receive. Once you do, you will find the structure liberating rather than constricting.

The structure of Vocal Awareness and Communication Mastery is absolute. In ballet, there is only one proper way to stand in first position. In Vocal Awareness and Communication Mastery, there is only one correct way to perform each element in the workout.

In the subsequent section, you will be learning the *mechanics* of the Work. As you do so, please also remember to remain in Stature. Do your best to incorporate Ritual 1, Thank You to My Source, and Ritual 2, Love and Let Go, as you continue learning and practicing each additional exercise. In all forms of Mastery, you can *never leave any pieces out*. Form and Structure are always required. At the conclusion of this section, you will know how to do the Work while consciously and seamlessly integrating the Rituals into everything you do.

Finding Your Stance

The first thing you need to do before you can begin your warm-up is to identify the appropriate stance that is best suited to you and that best supports the Work and you. One of the best ways to learn this is by experimenting with various positions until you find the correct one. As you will soon discover, the body has an innate intelligence and muscular memory. On a subconscious level, it retains information and even responds to the commands you give it. Granted some people are more in touch with their kinesthetic awareness than others, but everyone can become more conscious. With practice, it becomes easier to sense when you have shifted out of position and when to make the necessary adjustments.

The Vocal Awareness Method is nonexclusionary. It can be executed seated or standing. If you choose to or need to remain in your chair, simply follow the instructions skipping any indications to stand and then sit.

Let's begin. Try a brief exploration in front of a mirror. (For now, a mirror is the only tool you will need.) Stand up now if you plan to work on your feet. Otherwise, begin from your current position.

Without making any physical adjustments, notice your body language. Scan from your toes to the tip of your head and along your arms. Take in the entire picture. Do not change a thing as you get settled in. How does it feel?

Now, stand or sit in Stature feeling extraordinary about yourself. I do not ask that you believe it—yet. Just do it. Notice the difference. Does the room seem quieter? Do you feel any different inside? Can you recall the first thing your body did when you gave it the command: "Stand in Stature" or "Sit in Stature"? Observe that the body's response is to inhale.

Next, stand or sit at attention. What does it feel like? Did you breathe? No. This is not the correct posture for your workout because you are rigid. Your muscles are more constricted.

Again, stand or sit in Stature. Imagine a string gently pulling you up through the top of your head. Reflect a wonderful Self-admiring person—not arrogant, but instead embodying your persona. *Standing or sitting in Stature is not only a physical posture but also a state of mind.*

Stature—Pulling the Thread   **Stature**

I realize it may take a while to claim this new physical identity, however, it is critical to both your physical and emotional development to learn to be in Stature. Even if you don't fully understand and/or feel resistance, please do it anyway. Remember Vocal Awareness is integrating both the *inner* Voice and the outer voice congruently at all times and this integration is a foundation of Communication Mastery. In my teens and early twenties, I had very low Self-esteem, and standing in Stature seemed almost fraudulent. I stayed committed, and an internal shift resulted. I began to believe in myself, and, at that moment, *to be in Stature* became my natural state. Stature is the first step in sustaining your commitment to your Persona Statement.

In Stature, your head should be erect, your shoulders level, and your legs about a foot apart. Breathe naturally. If you are seated, your feet should be flat on the floor. It is important to be able to breathe freely and deeply in this stance and to feel a solid connection to the ground. Experiment by separating your legs to a greater distance. Then, place your feet together. Turn your toes straight ahead, then in, and then out. In which Stature do you feel the best and most confident? Some people find that putting one foot slightly forward as they stand actually helps them breathe more effectively.

The Jaw Release

Once you are standing or sitting in Stature, you are ready to learn how to perform the physical and sound-making dynamics of the Vocal Awareness Workout. The Jaw Release is a principal component of most of the exercises. It helps to eliminate any tension you may be holding in your tongue, jaw muscles, and temporal mandibular joints. You can locate the temporal mandibular joints by placing your fingertips in front of your ears and opening your mouth. The correct spot is where you feel a space opening up as your jawbones move.

In addition, the condition known as TMJ syndrome is occasionally related to the structure of your mouth and the alignment of your jaw. More often than not, it is caused by stress as we habitually create tension by tightening our tongue, jaw, neck, and shoulders; grinding our teeth; or holding our breath. What results is vocal and physical constriction, and it can be very painful. TMJ syndrome is never positive. What is perceived by others is fear, anxiety, rigidity, and so forth. The Jaw Release exercise will mitigate TMJ syndrome and enhance your vocal and communication possibilities as well as contribute to a positive perception by others.

When doing the Jaw Release exercise, your initial aim is to be able to extend your mouth open enough that you can fit three fingers stacked one on top of the other between your top and bottom rows of teeth. You will be using one hand positioned in a specific

Correct

Incorrect

way that I'll describe in a moment. Gently and consistently stretch your lower jaw downward. Please note: *never force your jaw open*. If at first you can only achieve a one-finger or two finger extension, work from there. Over time, your jaw will become more flexible as a result of this exercise.

Checking for Tongue and Jaw Freedom

To do the Jaw Release properly and effectively, form a "V" with your hand by spreading your thumb away from your forefinger. Rest your hand against the ledge of your chin, just below your mouth, with your thumb on one side of your jaw and your fingers against the other. Your chin will be in the exact center of the "V." Experiment with different hand positions so you can discover for yourself the specificity of this position. Raise your hand position an eighth of an inch. Lower it an eighth of an inch. Shift it slightly to the right and to the left. Then, bring it back to center. Doesn't this feel more secure? That's why the right position is not arbitrary as in first position for the ballet dancer; it is exacting and the only way to do it.

Now, use gentle pressure to ease your jaw downward until your mouth is open, released, and as comfortable as possible. Remember not to force the jaw extension or tighten your neck or shoulders. The tip of your tongue should be resting, lying forward and gently touching the back of your bottom teeth. Simply use the weight of your hand as a pulley. While remaining in Stature, employ the 3rd Ritual breathing in Conscious Awareness while sustaining your jaw release.

Check your mirror to see whether you are doing the technique correctly. Your head should be level. You never drop or raise it as you release your jaw. It remains perpendicular. The aim is to experience a complete lack of tension in your tongue, jaw, neck, and shoulders.

With practice, you'll find it quite easy to achieve a natural freedom in your Jaw Release exercise. Furthermore, since tension depletes energy, you will actually have more energy after doing the exercise. As a result, you'll experience a newfound power and confidence as you speak, which in turn will further enhance your Communication Mastery.

Implementing Ritual 3: Allow a Slow, Silent, Conscious, Loving Breath

In all forms of mastery, to be "natural" requires consummate practice. To be in Communication Mastery, among other things, breathing effectively is foundational and will become your "new normal."

Earlier you read, "breath is fuel." Now I will elaborate. Breathing calms and energizes the body. Effective breathing makes your voice stronger and helps you focus and harness your emotional energy.

In order to heighten your kinesthetic awareness, let's do another experiment. Begin by standing or sitting comfortably in Stature, erect and relaxed with a certain sense of dignity. Refrain from judging the process. *Take* a deep breath, as though it is the "top of the morning" and "it's great to be alive." Notice how it feels to inhale like this. Then exhale and relax.

Now, I want you to experience a different kind of a breath. This time, please respond to these specific thoughts during successive breaths. Note: please do not rush. Observe the 5th Ritual: Take My Time.

> ➤ **Allow a *silent* breath.** Now exhale. Notice the difference from the breath you first *took*. With your first breath, your chest rose and your abdomen constricted. When you allowed a breath, your abdomen and rib cage both expanded and you felt more open and relaxed.

> ➤ **Allow a *silent* and *loving* breath.** Now exhale. What differences do you notice? Do you breathe more deeply? Is your speaking voice a bit lower and your vocal energy more dynamic?

> ➤ **Allow a *Silent, Loving, Down-through-my-body* Breath.** Now exhale. Again, please take time to observe what changes are occurring. Is your internal space calmer and your external space quieter? When you speak, do you notice even more resonance and clarity in your sound? When looking in the mirror, you may even see your pupils have begun to dilate and your eyes sparkle a bit. This is one sign of your endorphin level rising and, especially in media moments, contributes to your being telegenic and connecting with your audience. The shifts may be subtle or obvious, but they are taking place.

The important distinctions when you breathe effectively in Ritual 3 will lead to a profound change in your voice and communication. To sustain this breath moment-to-moment does require Conscious Awareness. This, in turn, helps eliminate negative communication behaviors. In all forms of mastery, to be *natural* requires consummate practice. In your daily Vocal Awareness Workout, this breath takes five to seven seconds and *it is always slow and silent.* You

CLB—Conscious, Loving Breath

may breathe either through your nose or mouth. There is value in learning to do both.

Implementing Ritual 4: See the Edge and Arc of Sound

Begin Ritual 4 with the Jaw Release exercise. As previously stated, each time you begin a ritual or an exercise, please repeat all the steps. *Don't leave pieces out.* In this case, the Jaw Release exercise will help assure greater freedom in your tongue, jaw, neck, and shoulders while doing the following vocal exercises. Remember you are creating a new system that will lead to consummate self-awareness. Another critical reason for being as conscientious as I'm asking you to be refers to a Vocal Awareness axiom, "The routine is never routine."

I had a Skype lesson with one of my clients who lives in Europe and owns a global company. During our lesson, he candidly shared that he had not been doing his daily Vocal Awareness Workout for a few weeks because of challenges in his personal life that made him feel as though he was unable to bring the proper level of focus and commitment to the Work that he previously had. Basically, "I've been going through the motions," he said. We did the Rituals and exercises together. Within five minutes, he was back on track and gratified to recognize that, even though he was perhaps emotionally reluctant or resistant to working as hard as he had before, with my support, he was quickly back on track in an integral/integrative way. He had an important public event rapidly approaching, and he was pleased to know his voice, mental acuity, and confidence were restored. Part of the point is never to approach any of this Work like calisthenics, but always from a perspective that reinforcing leadership and Communication Mastery is always your goal.

The Hub of the Voice

Returning to Ritual 4, when you confirm that the tension from your jaw has been sufficiently released, remove your hand from your jaw and gently close your lips as you are going to begin to do a simple humming exercise called "Finding the Hub of Your Voice."

Now, initiate out loud the sound, *Hmm*, as nasally as possible following a Conscious, Loving Breath with no tongue or jaw tension. Please don't force your voice aggressively or make the sound too loud. As you are discovering how to do this exercise, it is important to not be too loud because you can inadvertently harm your voice as you are learning to coordinate all the elements. Each time you repeat this or any exercise, *never rush*. Using the Rituals, refocus and conscientiously begin again.

Take a moment to experiment with this hum. First, simply do it. Second, do it with your finger placed on your top lip right under your nose and initiate the sound again. The third time, refer to the photograph of the Edge and Arc and *place your fingernail on the edge of your top lip.*

In Vocal Awareness, this is called the "Nasal Edge." From this moment forward, please recognize that *the Edge is your anchor.* It is the perfect location to see sound leave your body and soar through the Arc. Please don't struggle to empirically understand this. Instead notice what you hear and feel—an immediate shift in resonance, vocal energy, and strength. Repeating this fundamental exercise as effectively as possible over and over again will not only enhance and stabilize your voice and delivery but will also imbue you with more confidence. As you discover how to consistently calibrate

Correct

Incorrect

and integrate this basic exercise, what will emerge is Communication Mastery.

The *Hub* of your Voice is your *core sound*. It is the ideal place to always speak from. By doing this simple but sophisticated exercise, even for only a few seconds before every key speaking moment then delivering your message while *seeing* the Edge and Arc, you will consistently express yourself energetically and vibrationally in the most authentic way possible. Please remember that sound is vibration. This concept is not esoteric, but factual. It is science.

To further support your understanding of the *hub*, see it, for example, as the hub of a bicycle wheel. The spokes of that wheel metaphorically represent our multiple subpersonalities—the business leader, departmental manager, HR director, assistant, job applicant, and more personally, husband, wife, life partner, friend, and so forth. We are all this and more, but what this exercise enables us to do as strategically as possible when speaking in public is communicate as congruently as possible through the voice we *choose* to speak with—the one that represents our Persona Statement.

As you become more effective at simply sustaining this sound *with your lips gently closed and with no tongue tension* and on a single pitch for five or six seconds, begin to explore the Hub of your Voice exercise on higher or lower tones and continue to sustain each pitch for five to six seconds. Ultimately, this will extend your vocal range and expression. Keeping your finger in position, practice two or three more hums and see if you can feel the Nasal Edge vibration. Always strive to express the sound as extremely nasally as possible. *Never speak nasally, but always exercise nasally.* Nasality will enhance the resonance of your voice which, in turn, will contribute to others perceiving you as embodying more authority and leadership strength. Effective nasal warm-ups correspond physically to jogging with ankle weights as nasality positively taxes the laryngeal muscles making them work harder in a positive way as ankle weights contribute to runner's leg strength.

Before moving on to the next exercise, the Yawn-Sigh exercise, please refine this one. Habitually, we all *speak from the neck up*. You are now learning to speak more intentionally, and integratively, and more effectively with your entire mind and body.

Notice, for example, how your voice changes when your fingernail and hand correctly represent the Edge and Arc. (Note: refer to the Arc of Sound photograph.) Remember not to tilt your head up or let it drop down, nor should you tighten your neck and shoulders. In addition, whenever you See the Edge and Arc of Sound, you will notice that your abdominal muscles are working harder. Everything in Vocal Awareness is reflected physiologically, (i.e., Stature opens the chest and helps ground the body more efficiently). A Conscious, Loving Breath expands the chest cavity but also releases tension in our pharynx, mouth, and tongue. Seeing the Edge and Arc of Sound makes the abdominal muscles work harder in a positive way and thus enables us to not only express ourselves from our core sound imagematically but from our core physiologically. In all traditions and physical training, the center of our bodies; known as the core, is three inches below the navel.

The Arc of Sound

As we have been discussing Ritual 4, See the Edge and Arc of Sound, I have been focusing primarily on the Nasal Edge. Now, we will focus on *seeing* the Arc of Sound. Ritual 4 is a powerful, visual image that will radically enhance your Communication Mastery. As you embed the Arc image, visualize a soaring ski jumper or a plane taking off. All aerodynamic processes are the same in these two examples as well as in throwing a ball or using your voice effectively. Scientifically, it is known as the Bernoulli Effect, but, for our purposes, all you need to do is *see our sound soar*.

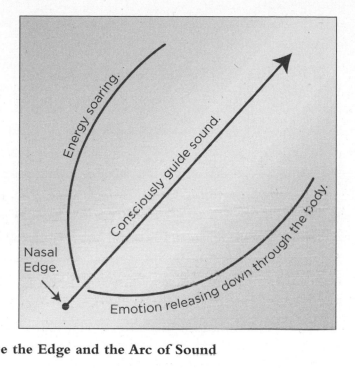

See the Edge and the Arc of Sound

To practice this, return to the Hub exercise but, instead of sustaining the same pitch, descend from that pitch, and rather than, *dropping off* simulating an arch, See an Arc. As a plane accelerates on take-off or a runner bursts out of the blocks, you will crescendo through the Arc. This will enable you to sustain the sound of your voice in a consistent and seemingly effortless manner. From this moment on, you will always *see your voice soaring even if pitch is descending.* In consummate Communication Mastery, this single exercise will enable you to no longer *speak to the last row of the house* in large public presentations as, among other things, it raises pitch. On television, you will not project your voice *out to the camera* as the result will be the same—pitch rises and you will appear strained and unnatural or drop your vocal energy. When you See the Edge and Arc of Sound, you will always be able to sustain your communication in the most consistent and effective way possible.

Besides the above visual examples, this experience is also akin to the concept of "follow-through." An athlete, for example, does not throw *at a target but rather through it*. In Communication Mastery, this exercise is the precursor to speaking *through* the end of a thought not *to* the end of a thought. This is the Vocal Awareness concept of "follow-through," which will be developed more thoroughly in Chapter 5.

Concluding this portion of Ritual 4, the Hub of your Voice, as you gain proficiency with this exercise and are able to effectively descend in pitch, practice speaking from where that pitch ends up. This is your authentic core sound in that moment, and as you learned at the beginning of this section, this singular exercise will enable you at anytime and anyplace to always embody your optimal voice.

The Yawn-Sigh Exercise

I know you are already inspired by what is occurring for you. Your voice is beginning to feel stronger and your communication more expressive. You are feeling more confident. Now, with the Yawn-Sigh exercise, you are about to take a quantum leap.

The Yawn–Sigh is the foundation of your Vocal Awareness Workout. You will be asked to do it in many variations from the initial Tongue Pull exercise, to Two-Fingers under the tongue, and the Pencil Technique. Through each variant, all of the principles remain the same.

As you begin, please be in Stature, sitting or standing in front of a mirror. Before beginning the exercise, please reference the Checklist. Next, place your hand on your jaw as you learned in the Jaw Release exercise.

Warm-Up 1: The Yawn-Sigh with Tongue Pull

For this exercise, you will be using a washcloth or handkerchief to gently pull your tongue down and out of your mouth as you

Tongue Pull

do the Yawn-Sigh. Don't use tissue or paper toweling because they'll stick to your tongue. The Tongue Pull enables you to experience an unobstructed sound as well as releases tongue tension.

As you pull your tongue down and out of your mouth, please do not grip it too hard or attempt to pull it too far. Simply take hold of your tongue with the cloth in your hand The cloth is important because it prevents your fingers from slipping. Steadily pull your tongue down and out of your mouth, without yanking on it.

Now, do the Yawn-Sigh exercise out loud, as nasally as possible with an aspirated "H" to precede the tone, with your hand to your jaw and gently pulling your tongue downward, on the sound of *Hah* as in "haaaat." Please *always* remember: do not force or rush any exercise. Again, the routine is *never* routine. As in the Hub exercise, see your sound crescendo through the Edge and Arc of Sound. As you practice the Jaw Release exercise in tandem with the Yawn-Sigh, it is your first opportunity to experience the benefit of what happens when you release tongue and jaw tension. Notice how your speaking voice changes after one Yawn-Sigh exercise. Through each exercise, you are incrementally ridding yourself of presentational bad habits that have impeded your ability to express yourself.

Before introducing a Yawn-Sigh variation, let's take a moment to observe what you have begun to do, but perhaps have not noticed or do not understand its benefits. First is the concept of the aspirated "H."

Perhaps you remember the character Eliza Doolittle in the play *Pygmalion* by George Bernard Shaw or in the musical *My Fair Lady* practicing her "H" sound in an exercise that Henry Higgins gave her. "Hurricanes hardly ever happen." The aspirated "H" sound propels the sound through the vocal folds.

Laugh for a moment (Ha Ha Ha). Did you hear how the "H" naturally preceded the tone? Using the breath in this manner gives your voice extra projection without straining your larynx/vocal folds. This principle should guide your exhalations throughout the vocal workout.

The second observation regards support. Physically, notice as you do a Yawn-Sigh exercise or speak through the Edge and Arc of Sound, your stomach muscles contract. This is physical support and is the fulcrum from which you project your voice. An additional interpretation of *support* is to be there for yourself. As you undertake these exercises, you are choosing to be there for yourself. Both interpretations of support are necessary for true Communication Mastery.

Warm-Up 2: The Two-Finger Yawn-Sigh

This exercise is identical to the Tongue Pull exercise except, instead of pulling your tongue gently down and out, you will be placing two fingers of one hand in your mouth under your tongue up to the first joint to encourage your tongue to lie forward and release any residual tension. Please relax your hand as you do so. Watching yourself do this in the mirror is helpful, as sometimes our tongues are quite unwieldy. Seeing how difficult it can be to merely let go makes it easier to release tongue tension.

All tension is fear-based. Where there is fear, there is doubt.

Now, do a Yawn-Sigh out loud, with your fingers under your tongue using the sound of *Hah* as in "haaaat." As before, encourage your pitch to descend slightly as you crescendo through the Edge and Arc of Sound. As always, the sound should be extremely nasally. Apply all the Rituals on the Vocal Awareness Checklist. Continue

Correct   **Incorrect**

using your hand to release your jaw (Another note: As you do all the exercises, *please do not spread your mouth.*)

There should be no visual effort. All the effort comes from your abdominal muscles.

As you do your daily Vocal Awareness Workout, you should feel no irritation in your throat. If you feel irritation in your throat such as tickles, scratches, or any kind of pain, your voice is telling you that you are doing something wrong. Your workout should never hurt. If there is discomfort, your tongue, jaw, neck, or shoulders may be too tight, your head may be elevated too high, your breathing may be rushed, your voice may be unfocused. It could be any one of these challenges or a combination of elements. The bottom line is to notice, not ignore, and do your best to figure out what is causing the problem. As you progress in your daily regimen, recognize that you are acquiring *complex* new skills that require attention to detail. (Note: not *complicated*. What makes it complicated is us—remember the KISS approach.) As you practice, please be aware that your emphasis should be on *excellence* not *perfection*. Striving to be perfect does not let you make mistakes and mistakes are inevitable. To strive for excellence requires mindfulness and puts the emphasis on being your best not your "perfect best."

Caution creates anxiety. Conscientiousness creates awareness.

Warm-Up 3: The Pencil Technique

Pencil Technique

In this exercise, you will be using your index finger or holding a pencil gently between your teeth as you do the Yawn-Sigh exercise. The previous versions enhance the size, color, and range of your voice. This exercise dramatically intensifies the focus and resonance of your voice enabling you to cut through every conversation like a laser beam and speak above the din without shouting, raising pitch, or hurting your voice. As you use a pencil, a Bic-type pen, or your index finger, please do not bite down hard. Therefore, do not try this exercise until you are confident that you will not tense your tongue and jaw while doing it.

Begin by standing or sitting in Stature. Place the pencil in your mouth, gently holding it just in front of your eyeteeth. There is no need to hold the pencil with your hands. Allow your tongue to lie comfortably behind the pencil and follow all the previous protocols.

As you get under way, take a moment to check for tension along the side of your jaw and in the soft spot on the underside of your chin, and release any tension you notice.

Now, do a Yawn-Sigh out loud, with the pencil in your mouth, on the sound of *Hah* as in

Pencil Technique with Index Finger

"Haaaat." Focus on projecting this sound extremely nasally *over the top* of the pencil (not under it or into it) and *way forward* in your mouth (i.e., the front of your hard palate).

The Three Aspects: The First Aspect

Earlier in this chapter, I introduced The Three Aspects. Now, as you have become familiar with the basic Vocal Awareness Workout, you will learn to integrate The Three Aspects in a pragmatic structure throughout everything you do. The Vocal Awareness Method is like a spider's web. It all begins to unravel when you remove a single strand. That's why attention to detail in all forms is so extremely vital, as the goal is always mastery. The web you are weaving to support that goal becomes as strong and resilient as a spider's web with the integration of mind/body/spirit.

In the First Aspect you are warming up, learning to take your time and to be conscientious. Never warm up *mechanically* or hear your vocalizations as *sound-making*. Rather, understand your Yawn-Sighs as emotional expression. As you vocalize, always do so with dynamic control—never too loud or too soft.

The Second Aspect: The Bridge

The Bridge is a powerful process that not only will enhance your Voice, it will also boost your confidence and enhance your technical proficiency. The Bridge will also, very importantly, enable you to be more Consciously Aware in every communication opportunity.

As teenagers, most of you took driving lessons. Early on you sat at the curb in the driver's seat with your instructor in the passenger seat. In the first lesson, you were taught to look in the rearview mirror and the driver's side mirror and to turn your head before tentatively pulling away from the curb. As you gained proficiency, you gained confidence. Several lessons later, you were driving on the open highway with a parent or instructor beside you. Fast forward 20 years. You wake up one day with the overwhelming urge to learn how to become a Formula One driver. You don't actually want to drive in a Formula One race, you just want to have the ability to drive that well on city streets and highways—you simply want to be a superb driver. To accomplish this, you enroll in Formula One classes such as the Bob Bondurant School of High Performance Driving. Several months later you graduate having fulfilled your goal of becoming an "expert" driver.

Up until this point, you have been in the Driver's Ed phase of this book. Instead of being taught how to look in the mirror and turn your head, you have been learning about your voice—how to breathe, how to warm up, and so on. The Bridge is the opportunity to achieve the goal of the driver who enrolled in a high performance driving school. Obviously, you are not learning how to be an expert driver; you are learning Communication Mastery. You are learning to be your very best as you discover how to navigate every meeting, every public presentation with the same expertise of a Formula One driver.

The Bridge is an original and unique rehearsal process. You can apply this phase of the Vocal Awareness Workout to any text or other *performance* material—what you may be preparing to say to your boss in asking for a raise or to a headhunter at a job interview, bullets for a PowerPoint presentation, or the opening paragraph of your keynote address. The Bridge/Second Aspect is designed to meticulously integrate technical proficiency with performance reality. The result—your mind/body/spirit will be more *consciously* in sync.

You are learning to become a master craftsman such as legendary artists and athletes—Meryl Streep, Kareem Abdul Jabbar, Georgia O'Keeffe, Jussi Björling, Wynton Marsalis, Mikhail Baryshnikov, and Gabriel Garcia Marquez. They hold themselves to the highest performance standards—and so can you. It is through The Bridge that you will develop your ability to do this. Once you learn how, Communication Mastery will reflect not just what you do but who you are.

Activity: The Bridge

For the purpose of learning how The Bridge works, you will practice the Tongue Pull, Two-Fingers Yawn-Sigh, and the Pencil Technique with the following text:

I am an extraordinary person and I do extraordinary things.

First, position yourself for the Tongue Pull exercise. Stand or sit in Stature. Place the Vocal Awareness Checklist where you can easily read it. Conscientiously apply the rituals and please make sure you have a recorder on. This is a *game film* opportunity.

Now, read the first line of the text aloud. Next, read it again while lightly pulling your tongue down in the same way that you made the sound Hah (haaaat) in the Yawn-Sigh exercise. Speak very slowly and extremely nasally by intensely elongating the phrase— without tension—extending the vowel sounds in an exaggerated manner. (To begin, you may practice the words one at a time rather than the entire phrase.) As this is a Yawn-Sigh with words, your goal, paradoxically, is not articulation but continuous focus and energy as in the Yawn-Sigh. *As you practice, if you understand one syllable, you are doing the exercise incorrectly.* While observing yourself in the mirror, please encourage your tongue to be as flaccid as possible. Your only goal is Conscious Awareness and sending this sentence soaring through the Edge and Arc.

Before moving on, employing Stature and Rituals 1 through 3, please say or read the sentence again as *naturally* as you can.

I am an extraordinary person and I do extraordinary things.

Now listen back to the first time you said the phrase and this time. You will hear a substantial difference—your voice is more resonant, stronger, and expressive; and your delivery sounds more confident. Metaphor: you appear more confident.

Next, repeat the exercise but with two fingers under the tongue. Stand or sit in Stature. Apply the Rituals and retrace every step. Read the text aloud, elongating the vowels and speaking very slowly and nasally:

I am an extraordinary person and I do extraordinary things.

Again, when you have finished, please listen back.

The third variation is the Pencil Technique. Before beginning, please refer to The Checklist paying particular attention to the 5th Ritual—Take My Time. Very often when doing repetitive exercises, you may begin to go *unconscious* and rush without noticing.

When you are ready, read the text, projecting your voice nasally *over the top of the pencil*:

I am an extraordinary person and I do extraordinary things.

Once again, please listen back. Do you notice more clarity, crispness, and a comfortable intensity in your delivery?

As you continue practicing, feel free to substitute any other text for the passage above. This exercise works equally well with PowerPoint bullets, a corporate or personal Mission Statement, and even common phrases you might find yourself using in social situations, such as "Hello, my name is . . . It's a pleasure to meet you, " a brief opening from your 'elevator pitch,' the first or closing paragraph from your keynote or others. Whatever statement or phrase you choose to use, please always practice in the mirror, refer to your Checklist, and record yourself. Remember, in all Mastery, "you cannot leave any pieces out." Communication Mastery is no different.

The Third Aspect: The Performance

You have arrived. It is time for you to put everything you have learned together in complete Conscious Awareness. In the Third Aspect, speak the same phrases you have been working on in The Bridge as authentically, mindfully, and naturally as possible. Before beginning, review your Persona Statement. This is your first opportunity to fully embody your brand in Communication Mastery. Please remember to record yourself.

Designing Your Daily Practice:
7 Minutes for 7 Days

Discover the value of the Vocal Awareness Method for yourself by practicing 7 minutes for the next 7 consecutive days. Strive to practice in the morning. With this commitment, you are enforcing an ethical commitment to yourself *to be your best*. As you do the Vocal Awareness Workout daily this week, you will notice substantive improvement in your ability to do the exercise as well as in its influence at work and in your daily life. In time, as your awareness grows, you can begin to develop your own customized Vocal Awareness Workout.

The following is a matrix for a sample 7-Minute Workout Routine. It is not necessary that you spend the 7 minutes of your practice session doing *exactly* these steps. However, it is important that your session include all three aspects of the Vocal Awareness Workout: The Warm-Up, The Bridge, and The Performance. Please always maintain Mastery Protocols, (i.e., working with the mirror and having your Checklist visible). These are the nonnegotiable elements that will enable you to make significant progress. In time your 7-minute routine will be determined by your specific needs.

A 7-Minute Workout

While standing in Stature (remember the *invisible thread*), do the following:

First Aspect

> **Minute 1:** Focus, review the 7 Rituals, center yourself.

> **Minutes 2 and 3:** A combination of the Tongue Pull, Two-Finger, and Pencil Technique Yawn-Sighs.

Second Aspect

> **Minute 4:** The Tongue Pull Yawn-Sigh with text.

> **Minute 5:** The Two-Finger Yawn-Sigh with text.

> **Minute 6:** The Pencil Technique Yawn-Sigh with text.

Third Aspect

> **Minute 7:** Performance.

Please feel free to expand the duration of your workout session. Seven minutes is the *minimum* guideline. Again, Vocal Awareness is *a being work, but we have to do to be.* Seven Minutes a Day is just that—being while doing. It combines preparation and practice resulting in consummate execution and communication excellence. Communication Mastery ultimately requires the consistent integration of mind/body/spirit. This is achieved by doing the Work, not merely reading the book.

Customizing Your Daily Routine

Even though the Vocal Awareness Workout has a specific structure, your daily workout routine has a certain amount of flexibility. There are variations on the exercises that you can try as your technical abilities become stronger. Please be aware that as your practice sessions become a regular part of your day, *the routine should never become routine.* You are breaking longstanding, *unconscious* behaviors and ineffective vocal habits. Always stay focused and alert. This is Conscious Awareness.

At the beginning of a session, set a specific intention about what you are going to work on, such as any one of the 7 Rituals (e.g., *See the Edge and Arc of Sound* or *Take My Time*). Ideally, every session can be creative, unique, and rewarding. Enjoy the discoveries, expanding your horizons, and your commitment to the Work.

Action Step ··········➤

First, commit to 7 Minutes for 7 Days.

At least once in the first 7 days, strive to incorporate what you have learned in your daily practice at work. It could be a phone call, a visit with a colleague, a prepared meeting, walking down the hall in Stature, stopping before going into a meeting to focus your attention, or embodying your Persona. Whatever you choose to do, it is your opportunity to apply what you are learning.

Regularly update your journal with the discoveries you have made, any possible challenges you have recognized, and the accomplishments you have achieved.

5

THE MESSAGE AND THE MESSENGER: IT IS NOT JUST DATA. IT IS COMMUNICATION.

The medium is the message.

—Marshall McLuhan

It is not just the message, but the messenger that matters.

A s a society we must confront one of the gravest societal challenges of the twenty-first century: losing the art of public discourse, what it truly means *to speak with* one another—to communicate.

Before proceeding with this chapter, please glance at the cover of the book and reread the title. In Chapter 4, you learned the mechanics of Communication Mastery. In this chapter, you will learn how to embody your technique in order that the *message* and the *messenger* are *always* inextricably linked. Remember the goal of Vocal Leadership is for the *same person* to show up everywhere in full Conscious Awareness, *communicating the message*—never just distilling data. The word *communication* comes in part from the Latin *communicare*—to share, join, or unite. The word *data* comes from the Latin *datum*—a piece of information.

With the advent of the Internet, we rely on *fingers and thumbs* and instant messaging to speak to one another. When we type, no one hears our actual voice—the sound of who we are—our identity. In a way, we are anonymous. However, as a society we have not as of yet devolved into a population where verbal discourse is no longer required. For some this may be comforting, but it is insidious as it is still necessary for everything we do—but we are clearly less practiced at it. A PowerPoint presentation does not deliver itself. A board meeting requires members to sit at a conference table interacting with one another. In sales, cold calling requires us to speak to a customer. An interview necessitates dialogue. In every business encounter, every media moment, as we share, as we lead, we unconsciously reveal *everything* about who we are. We reveal subliminal messages about inner strengths or personal weaknesses, but *perception is always reality*. It does not matter what is true. All that matters is *what our audience perceives as truth*. Every aspect of our communication—verbal or nonverbal—communicates *our truth*; the pitch and tone of our voices, our breathing patterns, our body language, facial expressions, speed of delivery, vocal energy, dynamics, and so on. The point is, we send *signals* through our body's "broadcast system" whether we are aware of it or not. In this chapter, we will confront head-on the tactical necessity of recognizing that *it is not only what we say but how we say it and deliver it that matters.* Ownership of the message and the messenger enhance our actual leadership prowess. Incorporating the techniques you are learning will not only help you astutely convey your message but also help you to no longer speak *to* one another, but rather to effectively speak *with* one another. That is true co—mmunication!

The bottom line is that all business decisions are influenced by how we are perceived. This is not merely a turn of a phrase, but a fresh interpretation on the perennial axiom—the bottom line.

When we watch actors play a part, they become their character, which only has to be sustained for that film, play, or TV show. But in business and throughout our lives, there is no script to follow, and no lines to read. We don't have a character to play; we only have our Self. We don't have a director helping us understand how to play our parts. If we have not clearly defined the character being played, our Persona, we cannot determine what we want our audience to see or know about us. Therefore, the expectations of the audience are projected onto us. This complicates each interaction as we strive to meet their demands, expressed or not. This unconscious interface is a key driver in the traditional presentational matrix.

Now, let's shift the paradigm. Do not think in terms of presentation, rather think in *performance* terms. From this point forward, the commitment is not to *present* one's self, but to *be* one's Self. *Understand that every public encounter is a performance because someone is watching.* Do not misconstrue performance as theatrical and inauthentic, but instead as responsible and tactical.

Another paradigmatic shift in thinking is required to maximize every performance opportunity. Traditionally, employees strive to fulfill their potential. In Communication Mastery, one no longer strives to fulfill potential, but seeks to be our very best—to achieve. Potential comes from the Latin root *posse* meaning in part "possible." In other words, potential reflects possibility. The word *achieve* means to "perform successfully." It is related to the word *chief*. To be in Mastery, not only Communication Mastery, requires you step in and step up in every way. Commit to no longer fulfilling your potential, rather to *achieving your possibility*.

Arnold and Paul

Arnold

In 1982, I received a phone call from a noted Hollywood agent asking me to train Arnold Schwarzenegger. This call prompted the beginning of one of the more significant Vocal Awareness chapters of my life. I worked with Arnold or several years throughout numerous movies, including his first major film, *Conan the Barbarian.* It was clear we came from two different walks of life, but our drive for excellence was identical.

As I often say in Vocal Awareness, "When you give me your Voice, you give me who you are." The goals are always professional; the process is often quite personal. Components that are integral to the process are mutual trust, dedication, and revelation. In business the principles are the same. In this case, working with a consummate champion meant that he would never settle for less than being his best—he was accustomed to mastering one skill, scaling hurdle after hurdle, and he always saw a challenge instead of an obstacle. This held true regardless of whether his role was of athlete, actor, entrepreneur, businessman, or governor.

From our first Vocal Awareness session, I clearly remember my strategic decision to not rid Arnold of his accent. Instead, the focus was to develop his entire voice—strengthening it, enhancing its size, and bringing more presence, vocal color, articulatory clarity, and emotion to every character he portrayed. The strategy was designed to match the character of the voice to the character/persona the audience saw portrayed on the screen.

We have already discussed that structuring time is fundamental to achieving success and personal Mastery in any discipline. Arnold's daily routines, his regimen, followed for decades in the gym were also applied to every aspect of his career. As an athlete, he established a vision, a mission, and goals. He worked tirelessly to achieve them. As an entrepreneur and political leader, the criteria were the same. Instead of training to be Mr. Olympia, he strenuously prepared for every part, and his political path was years in the making.

Paul

I had been consulting with a Fortune 100 company for many years when I first met Paul at corporate headquarters. Paul had risen through the ranks and, prior to my meeting with him, had recently been appointed COO. Paul knew I had been working with the company's CFO and Paul stopped in one day to ask me if I would train him as well. A long and fulfilling relationship began.

A year into his Vocal Awareness training, Paul was asked to speak at a prestigious, industrywide conference. We had six months to prepare. My first request was that Paul write out his entire speech. He did so, calibrating it with his Persona and Vision Statements. We then spent several weeks retooling. Three months out, Paul began memorizing—verbatim. Two months out, we began rehearsing and paraphrasing on camera. This practice enabled him to be more extemporaneous and not robotic when in performance. Each session was preceded by the Vocal Awareness Workout. In addition, Paul's performance voice had always been a bit monochromatic—lacking in vocal strength and expression. To surmount this, he began studying singing with me. This significantly enhanced the power, range, and color of his voice. He also enjoyed his singing lessons immensely.

The month before he was to give his speech, we practiced diligently every week and employed the entire Vocal Awareness arsenal. When studying his *game film*, Paul began to recognize when he may not have been in Stature or perhaps dropped the Edge and Arc. Those performance lapses were rectified in the rehearsals that followed.

During the last week of preparation, I introduced one critical element often overlooked during the rehearsal process. I asked Paul to arrive at the venue two days early, rehearse in the space with his PowerPoint slides on his laptop, and record rehearsal. He was also asked to locate the sound engineer and request a lavaliere microphone that would leave him free to stand center stage.

The day of the event arrived. All other corporate leaders who spoke stood moribund at the podium—being business leaders delivering their PowerPoint. Paul embodied Communication Mastery—embodying a leader in business—and was the only one standing center stage wearing a lavaliere mic. He made the cover of the industry's international trade publication; Paul is now the CEO.

Storytelling: Moving from Messaging to Engagement

From this point forward, you are no longer a presenter. You are a performer. In this context, you will no longer convey data. You will learn how to tell your story and the company's story. Whatever the message may be, as the messenger, you will now learn to tell your tale.

For a number of years I was a consultant to Walt Disney Imagineering. My responsibility was to teach artists, designers, writers, and others how to tell stories. Senior management recognized that the talent could create the product, but they were not effective at selling the product. The following is the blueprint of what became known as "Vocal Awareness Storytelling."

Storytelling is a profound archetype for the human condition. Stories tap into man's four basic emotions—anger, fear, sadness, and joy. They reveal who we are. Their universality is due in part to their psychological insights and moral teachings. *To tell a story is to be human.*

You may be asking, why does this knowledge matter? At work I am not required to be a great storyteller and spin a yarn. I'm required to be diligent and good at my job. According to a longtime client and dear friend, Karen Dietz, PhD, former executive director of the National Storytelling Network and the leading curator in the nation on business storytelling:

> *Storytelling is not simply about messaging. It is instead all about relationships. . . . Storytelling at the very basic transactional level [requires] that you tell a story, [someone] listens, and if [you have done your job well], [they] will buy [your] product or service. . . . When we listen to somebody's story and tell ours in return, we are promoting a relationship. An authentic relationship that also builds trust. And, isn't that what we want in business? Building trust with [our] customers and building loyalty.*
>
> *The next best kind of storytelling is at the transformational level. This is where, every time I tell a story, I get to learn something new—about me and about you—and, hopefully, you get to learn something, too. This is where storytelling becomes a constant source of inspiration—where we get to tap into our creativity, express ourselves authentically."[1]*

Traditionally, storytellers understand the requisite listening skills required to be a consummate storyteller. Listening allows you to hear the stories around you. This, in turn, enables you to know which stories to tell your audience. Beyond this, Vocal Awareness will introduce the third paradigm in this chapter—the principles of the 6th Ritual: Pay Attention/Deeper Listening as applied to your storytelling responsibilities.

Dr. Dietz has one more critical piece of advice to share regarding the four basic stories that would be most effective to tell in your daily business life:

1. **Your Founding Story.** This is the story of how you got started in your work. What choices did you make? What hurdles did you have to overcome? What problem are you trying to solve?

2. **People and Results Stories.** These are stories about the people in your company, or the people you work with, and the obstacles they have overcome to satisfy customers. They can also be stories about your customers and how their lives are different because of what you have helped them accomplish.

3. **Your Future Story.** This is the story about what your customers want to become. It's also the story about the future that you and your customers are cocreating together because of your relationship. For example, the company Patagonia is deeply committed to sustainability. They are very bold about the kind of future that they are focused on creating, and they share a number of stories that tell of the kind of future they are creating with their customers.

4. **Your Commitment Story.** This is a story about why you get up in the morning, every morning, to do the work that you do. People want to know they can trust you and that you are dependable. They want to know what keeps you going when times are tough. If you are asking them to commit to you by buying a product or service of yours, they want to know your commitment to them in return.

If you are a leader in an organization, there are a few additional stories that you are going to want to tell. If you are focused mostly on marketing, you will probably tell more People and Results Stories. If you're focused on using stories for job interviews and career advancement, there is a different set of stories you are going to want to tell. At some point, your audience is going to want to know how you got started, what your future story is, and your commitment story—regardless of [how you apply the] stories.[2]

In business, there is always a goal and a reason for telling a story, regardless of what the story is. The most ubiquitous story is known as a call to action. The following is an example:

"This amazing little device . . . is the size of a deck of cards . . . It only weighs 6½ ounces . . . It is ultra-portable . . . It has Apple design . . . a stainless steel back . . . It's durable . . . [It]holds 1000 songs and goes right in my pocket."[3] In a matter of moments, the audience was transfixed. Steve Jobs knew the iPod launch was a sales platform. The way he told the story prompted millions of people to rush to get in line to purchase an iPod. Instead of describing form and function as a technology leader, Steve Jobs created a storytelling narrative.

Visceral Language

You are about to learn one of the single most important communication techniques you will ever need to know—*how to make Voice visual*. In Vocal Awareness, this is called Visceral Language, which is *conveying the emotion of words*. It is a transformative principle of Communication Mastery that makes it possible for you to be in Conscious Awareness in every message you deliver and every story you tell.

Some time ago, I was invited to lead a seminar at the Wharton School of the University of Pennsylvania. In my opening remarks I said:

"You are the future leaders of our global society." Note: I am not qualifying this statement by describing you only as "business leaders" rather as "leaders," for what you do can change the world. The education you are receiving equips you to make a difference.

William James's inspiring challenge says it best, "The great use of a life is to spend it for something that outlasts it."

This statement will now become the framework for Visceral Language. As you undertake this segment of the Work, remember everything you are learning is designed to support your commitment to Communication Mastery. Through earlier examples that referenced athletic or artistic prowess, what is always implicit is what Malcolm Gladwell in *Outliers* called "the 10,000 hours rule."[4] To paraphrase: to master a skill, one repetitively practices that skill for 10,000 hours. Again, connecting this axiom to two fundamental principles of all mastery—the requirement to master the subtleties of form and integrating mind/body/spirit is essential. This understanding is critical as you acquire and integrate the techniques of Visceral Language.

Whenever you practice this new discipline, you need to first complete your Vocal Awareness Workout. The Workout can be abbreviated, but it cannot be eliminated. Again, each time you practice you are strengthening laryngeal muscles, eradicating negative behavioral habits, and attuning your nervous system. Always remember: *Nothing in Vocal Awareness is ever linear—it is always integrative.* Nowhere is that more apparent than when practicing Visceral Language. These techniques synthesize all the elements required for consummate Communication Mastery. When successful, they epitomize Conscious Awareness.

Making Voice Visual

Even if you do not read music, when learning to sing a song, the art is in interpreting the visual within the structure of the music. The musical page will tell you everything you need to know—at what pitch to sing each syllable or word, how loud or soft to sing it, when to crescendo or decrescendo, how to interpret the lyric, what style to sing in, which tempo to use, and so on. The framework is completely visual. On the other hand, actors only have words—a script with perhaps a few stage or camera directions. At the very most, the playwright or screenwriter will contribute subtextual background to orient the actor. Improvisation is different because performers do not have a script. Their training has prepared them to be fully *present* in the moment. Although they may not know exactly where they are going, they are not unconscious going there. We are all improvisational performers. Every day, virtually every moment of our lives is unscripted.

Once again, this brings to mind the Vocal Awareness axiom: *Structure does not impinge, it liberates. Freedom without direction is chaos.* Visceral Language combines the spontaneity of an unscripted performance with visual acuity. From this moment on, whether in a prepared speech, spontaneous conversation, or critical interview, the following guidelines and template will visually support you and mentally focus you at all times.

The paragraph below from the Wharton School seminar will now be annotated in Visceral Language. You will discover that although you don't know what the markings mean, you will subconsciously interpret the speech in a more effective way than you would have without the visual guidelines. Following it is a handwritten annotated version and symbol explanation.

> *"You are the future leaders of our global society." Note: I am not qualifying this statement by describing you only as "business leaders" rather as "leaders," for what you do can change the world. The education you are receiving equips you to make a difference. William James's inspiring challenge says it best, "The great use of a life is to spend it for something that outlasts it."*

"You are the future leaders of our global society." Note: I am not qualifying this statement by describing you only as "business leaders" rather as "leaders," for what you do can change the world. The education you are receiving equips you to make a difference. William James's inspiring challenge says it best, "The great use of a life is to spend it for something that outlasts it."

Visceral Language

Symbol Explanation

1. **CLB = Conscious, Loving Breath**

   This is a slower, deeper, and whenever possible, silent breath. This acronym will remind your unconscious mind to slow down when necessary and will enable you to have more *thinking time* and control. In addition, CLB helps contribute to more vocal strength, expression, and confidence.

2. **/ = A Downbeat**

   This is a musical term. Where you see the downbeat, your unconscious mind will put greater stress—emphasis—on a vowel or syllable. This will, in turn, contribute to your communicating with more authority and enhanced communication dynamics.

3. **✔ = A Catch Breath**

   This is the most fundamental breath we use in everyday conversation, and most often within paragraphs and storylines of prepared speeches. Our habit is we never notice a breath. Particularly in prepared texts, it is imperative to do so in order for the delivery to be as conscious and *natural* as possible. Without this visual reminder, you will forget to breathe in the most appropriate places. Remembering the earlier admonition—*breath is fuel*—you will always run out of gas.

4. **= the 4th Ritual—"To See the Edge and Arc of Sound."**

This image contributes to maximizing resonance and vocal strength, both critical to performance stamina.

5. ⊙ : *See* **the Punctuation**

Everytime you stop, even if it is not a complete thought, *literally*—not merely figuratively—*see a period!* This could be a difficult concept to grasp, but it is definitely worth the effort.

Each time you see a period, your voice and delivery will convey more definition and strength. Your thought will not trail away—*seeing the period* will enable you to *follow through*. (Remember in Vocal Awareness, we do not speak *to* the end of a thought, we speak *through* the end of a thought.) In addition, the listener/audience's perception is that you are more authoritative and confident.

6. **Underlining = Emphasis**

Underlining a consonant or a word reminds you to stress that word or sound. This enhances resonance and contributes to more effective articulation, enunciation, and expression. Your message will be clearer and your audience will perceive you as well spoken.

7. **T = Transition**

   This is the connective tissue of storytelling. A transition alerts the unconscious mind of the listener to pay attention. Wherever you place the "T" mentally in spontaneous communication or visually in prepared text, the next phrase will be conveyed with different emphasis. Where the "T" is placed, you may choose to speed up or slow down, be louder or softer, and so on. It is employed when you want to make a definitive point or create a transition to a new thought.

8. **W = What?**

   This is a technique I created many years ago for broadcasters. I have always explained it by saying—"the W/the what" represents a question. Where there is a question, there must be an answer. It helps us listen better.

Practice reading the first sentence of the paragraph annotated in Visceral Language. Where the *W* is inserted, say the word *what* and the subsequent word. "You are—*what?*—the future leaders of *what?*—our global society." Next read the line and hear where the *what* goes without reading it aloud. Please note: this does not mean you pause each time you see a "W." This simple technique refines your listening skills better enabling you to be in Conscious Awareness moment to moment, like great improvisational performers.

Marking the Text: Bringing the Words to Life

Once again, please read the following paragraph aloud. If possible, record yourself.

"You are the future leaders of our global society." Note: I am not qualifying this statement by describing you only as "business leaders" rather as "leaders," for what you do can change the world. The education you are receiving equips you to make a difference. William James's inspiring challenge says it best, "The great use of a life is to spend it for something that outlasts it."

Before reading the statement aloud a second time as it is annotated in Visceral Language, first review your Vocal Awareness Checklist. After reviewing, read the statement to yourself, striving to interpret the Visceral Language annotation. When you are relatively confident that you understand, please read aloud and record.

Visceral Language

After you have recorded yourself, please listen to your recording. You should definitely hear greater expression, sense more vocal energy and personal authority—overall, this is a more authentic and embodied delivery.

I recently had the privilege of working with a client who is often identified as one of the most significant business leaders in the world. Part of our work is designed to help him transition out of the implicit role of being a highly successful business leader into that of being a *leader in business*. The pivot point was a 40-minute keynote speech I was helping him prepare for a major university colloquium. To date, the presentation would be the longest of his career. The speech was 60 pages double-spaced. Two days immediately prior to the event, we spent a great number of hours together in preparation.

Our sessions included comprehensively annotating the entire speech in Visceral Language, rehearsing it multiple times on camera, and reviewing. When he delivered his address, everything he had envisioned achieving both personally and professionally was accomplished. Personally—he fully embodied the leader he is in consummate Conscious Awareness. I had said to him in an e-mail the day of the event, "This is a bold speech. You must be bold delivering it." Professionally—the media response was overwhelmingly positive and the message he was sending resoundingly received. Frankly, the degree of success would not have been possible without the visual structure of Visceral Language.

Visceral Language enables you to be in Communication Mastery. When applied to maximum effect, the results are quite remarkable. *Visceral Language is the game changer.* When using this technique, not only is your voice more resonant, your vocal and physical energy more consistent, your storytelling more effective, but you appear to be, and actually are, more confident, "natural," definitive, trustworthy, and so forth. Most important, you have control of both *the message and the messenger*, and that is a fundamental tenet of all leadership—to be in charge.

Before putting it all together, there are two more elements to discuss—space and speed. Please take a breath. Now *allow* a breath.

Notice your internal and external space. You have discovered that, in the latter, your environment is quieter; you are subtly more aware, energized, and relaxed. This *environment* is a prerequisite which activates the 6th Ritual of Vocal Awareness—Pay Attention/ Deeper Listening. The refinement of Deeper Listening not only enables you to hear better, but to *listen* with greater acuity. Deeper Listening helps you to *tune out* and *tune in* simultaneously. As you integrate this skill, you are better able to focus on what you are capable of hearing, internally and externally. You also become more effective at negating sights and sounds that emotionally or auditorially disrupt or distract you.

According to Dr. Seth S. Horowitz, PhD, an auditory neuroscientist at Brown University:

> *Listening is a skill that we're in danger of losing in a world of digital distraction and information overload. And yet we dare not lose it. Because listening tunes our brain to the patterns of our environment faster than any other sense, and paying attention to the nonvisual parts of our world, feeds into everything.*[5]

In this more receptive *space* of Deeper Listening, we are better able to not just hear our words, but also hear the emotions carried in the harmonics of everything we say. This ability is fundamental to *principled leadership*—communicating with integrity—in a way that others not only hear your words, but are compelled and inspired by your ideas and who you are.

One additional thought about space. A number of years ago a client returned from a leadership boot camp. Among other things, he was excited to show me how he learned to *pause* at appropriate intervals when delivering a speech. I said, "I don't want you to create pauses; I want you to create *space*. Space has value. A song without a rest—a space—is not the same piece of music." He proceeded to test this concept and discovered that when he enforced a *pause* in his delivery, he sounded less natural, more rushed, and his pitch became elevated. In contrast, when creating a *space*, his breath was a bit fuller, his pitch was lower, and when listening back, he discerned that he sounded more authentic and less presentational—more himself. Again, *Mastery is in the subtlety*.

I have been saying for decades, *"Speed is only speed. It is never how fast our communication, rather how effective. Nothing is gained by going too fast, but potentially everything could be lost."* As you have learned, *speech is habit*. We do not think about it, we just do it. In Communication Mastery, you are learning to think about it while you do it. To do so embeds a new habit—a new behavior. Nowhere is this more critical than in being able to recognize when you *speak too fast*.

When I taught the noted motivational speaker Tony Robbins, he referred to the Vocal Awareness Rituals as "pattern interrupts." He said, "You have to interrupt an old pattern to establish a new one." The 5th Ritual—Take My Time—does exactly that. As you begin to slow down, you break old patterns and establish new ones. Being mindful of *space and speed* allows you to gain *thinking time—control*. This allows you to be better able to convey each message on *your* terms.

Before ending this section, please create your own paragraph and annotate it in Visceral Language. This will take a little practice but it is worth the effort. Once you have clarified what you want to say, annotate it to the best of your ability. To prepare, use your Ritual Checklist, the daily Vocal Awareness Workout, and pay special attention to the Second Aspect. Always remember the principles of *space and speed* and record yourself delivering your text. As always, remember this is a course in Mastery. Please notice subtle distinctions—for example, possibly rushing, shallow breaths, or not *seeing* periods. Your goal is to embody your Persona. In other words, to *Be Your Self*.

Action Step ··········▶

Remember, a champion does it differently. With each chapter, you are acquiring clearer insight, learning practical exercises, and gaining greater understanding. Please write a 30-second presentation (just one paragraph) and annotate it in Visceral Language. This could be the opening or closing 30 seconds of an important PowerPoint presentation, your standard pitch or elevator speech to customers, or a statement about yourself that would be germane to a critical interview. Whatever you choose to write, it is important that it have meaning for you. As you do this Action Step, remember that *Structure does not impinge, it liberates.* As you need to, reference relevant sections of this chapter to remind yourself how to write your opening and practice it as effectively as possible. Your goal at this point of the journey is to begin to recognize *how to be*—and *what it is to be*—in Communication Mastery.

6

THE PERFORMANCE: OUR AUDIENCE IS OUR SELF

*Each man must look to himself to teach him the meaning of life.
It is not something discovered: it is something molded.*

—Antoine de Saint-Exupery

t is impossible for me to write this chapter and not reflect on the impact Vocal Awareness has. I saw this impact on four separate occasions during one single week. In the nearly five decades I have devoted to this Work, this week ranks among the top five most significant weeks I have ever experienced.

To begin the week, one of the most impactful business leaders in America had three highly successful media/public events and was definitively in Communication Mastery both when scripted and unscripted. The public response on Twitter, via e-mails, and across all media platforms was overwhelmingly affirmative. This individual was referred to me two years prior by another executive I had been working with for eight years. I had also helped shepherd his colleague through three career advancements. At this point, he is the third ranking leader in his organization.

When we first began to work, he was already exceedingly successful and highly regarded. What originally compelled him to seek training was his innate desire to always improve himself in everything he does. Public speaking was never something he enjoyed doing, but something he had to do. He said to himself, "Let me master that." Subliminally, he also recognized that as he raised the bar for himself he raised the bar for everyone else in the corporation.

From our first session he allowed significant access. Everything was on the table. We discussed family, friends, colleagues, business goals, our mutual histories. I sat in on staff meetings, occasionally listened to conference calls, took copious notes, and recorded lessons and group meetings. A strategy emerged. In Chapter 3, I spoke about the implicit trust between Lionel Logue and King George VI. In this case, I was rewarded with the same degree of trust.

Interrupting this narrative for a moment, it is important to understand that trust is not necessarily established because of a strong referral or the fact that we may convey cogent ideas or appear bright and knowledgeable of our subject matter. The level of trust I am speaking of is when another individual truly allows full access, and we allow the same across a range of ideas and conversations that are natural and honest. This trust is created through another's intuitive connection with us. It is subliminal—conveyed from one to the other not just in what we say but how we say it— through our voice, body language, expression, and so forth. If I had met with him and felt personally insecure and lacking confidence in any way, or presented a persona that reflected "I hope you approve" rather than embodying the integrity of who I am, this and so many other critical relationships in my life would never have come to fruition.

With trust established and a game plan in place he learned and continues to do the same things that you are being taught in this book—the same Vocal Awareness Workout, goals setting, creating timelines, and accountability to deliverables. Through the efficacy of the Work and his integral commitment to do whatever it takes, he reaps enormous personal and professional benefits. At this writing, the strategy that we put in place for his growth is now beginning to be extrapolated throughout the organization.

During the same week, I received an e-mail from a television executive acknowledging the contribution Vocal Awareness is making at his network, both with executives and broadcasters. Again the point is: Communication Mastery is not task specific. It is human centric. The same Vocal Awareness principles apply in any business. They are in cross-cultural alignment through all levels of an organization. I was originally hired to train broadcasters for this network, but word got around (as invariably happens) and, after a period of time, the Work began to proliferate beyond the initial mandate.

I received yet another e mail from a client informing me that her corporation was moving ahead with a leadership proposal she had submitted. She explained that over the next five years, her proposal would change the internal nature of the organization and would help clarify the public's perception externally. The strategy that she sold to senior leadership included a number of Vocal Awareness principles from *embodying the brand to integrity/integration*. Over the past year, we have assiduously worked in biweekly sessions, both in person and on Skype. Her Persona has been effectively crafted, which enables her to embody her brand. Her next step is to support the individuals in her department to do the same. Our success is due to her integral commitment to herself and her vision of excellence. In turn, her staff feels ennobled by her. (Ennobling is a key attribute of Integrative Leadership that will be discussed in greater detail in Chapter 7.) Her staff are more vested and imbued with greater confidence. Ultimately, "they do a better job."

The final e-mail of the week came from a client at a multinational consulting and financial services firm in the United States. He notified me that the company had placed him in charge of a substantial governmental project valued at tens of millions of dollars. In my client's note he acknowledged the value of Vocal Awareness/Communication Mastery. Specifically, his Persona Statement enabled him to be more confident, and the Daily Vocal Awareness Workout helped him step into his new leadership role seamlessly integrating both *the message and the messenger.*

The principles and exercises you are learning in this book directly contributed to their successes. In every instance, each leader's commitment to the Vocal Awareness matrix—specifically, practicing the daily Vocal Awareness Workout in preparation for presentations was key. Most importantly, being in Conscious Awareness when they walked into the performance space, remembering to be in Stature and "finding the hub of their voices" enabled them to speak with more resonance, enhanced vocal dynamics, and personal authority.

The point of opening the chapter in this way is to address, both personally and professionally, how gratifying it is to see individuals stepping into their power and, through Communication Mastery, achieving demonstrable success. The broader point is that what the audience sees, whether one-on-one or a media audience of millions, is they are being themselves. Each performance is prepared, practiced, and implemented as strategically and meticulously as the most effective business plan. The audience affirmatively responds to their authenticity—reflected through the integrity of their Persona and the way they communicate their message. Without their doing the Work, the audience may not.

The focus of this chapter is *how much work it takes to be ourselves in public—while the public watches* and then adding the remaining details of the Vocal Awareness stratagem—body language and the principle of self-correction. Each of the leaders identified above worked diligently on understanding, practicing, and integrating these elements into both who they are and what they do. The successful assimilation of the techniques resulted in their ability to fully embody themselves in consummate Communication Mastery.

Body Language—the Body Speaks

As we get under way, I am compelled to remind you of two phrases stated periodically throughout this book—*speech is habit* and *we don't know what we don't know*. Once again you are learning Communication Mastery. This concept is a paradigm shift that requires prescient understanding and, to the best of your ability, consistent attention to each and every detail. It is not simply *business as usual*. As with each facet of the Work you have been practicing and learning, it is discovering the difference between taking a breath or *allowing a breath,* or the substantive vocal and energetic results when you truly *See the Edge and Arc of Sound*. Recognition of the axiom, *mastery is in the subtlety*, must always be paramount.

When speaking about body language, please do not merely read the words believing you understand. Do not simply *go through the motions* thinking you are doing it right. Take time to sit, stand, walk, speak, gesture, or even shake hands in front of a mirror. Your handshake is important, as it is often the first point of contact in any face-to-face meeting. Combined with warm and sincere eye contact, your handshake should be firm but not overbearing as it communicates self-confidence and openness. Whether you are greeting someone on the telephone, in the initial moments of a business meeting, or shaking someone's hand, the first three seconds of any encounter are critical. Remember, *an opinion is created in three seconds* and those first three seconds *speak volumes*.

Please always observe the myriad subtle and not so subtle distinctions as you apply all you have learned to this point. Again, Vocal Awareness is a *being Work, but we have to do to be.*

The White Noise of Body Language

In this section of the book, you will learn how to *fine tune the body's broadcast system.* To this point, we have been speaking in part about your "vocal" voice. Now I will speak about the language of your "body's" voice and the subliminal and direct messages your body transmits. At the conclusion of this chapter, your goal is to be aware of the synchronicity of your message—in all aspects of communication—mind/body/spirit.

Make a personal to-do list of physical behaviors that do not adequately reflect your Persona Statement—for example, you may fidget; tap your toes in a meeting; while sitting, nervously shake your leg; drum your fingers on the desk; have poor posture; grind your teeth; look stressed, anxious, or nervous; bite your fingernails; avoid eye contact; use repetitive gestures; or walk too quickly in the hallways. Conversely, make a similar list of behaviors that would positively contribute to your persona—breathing consciously; maintaining eye contact; a warm facial demeanor; being well groomed; being in stature as you sit, stand, and walk; or have a comfortable stride and pace as you move about your workplace.

From this point forward please substitute self-correction for self-criticism/judgment. You are developing a critical skill—to observe yourself with a discerning and objective eye. Experiment in the mirror with an audio recorder or camera speaking the paragraph or theme you created in the previous chapter. You will perhaps notice that each time you begin both walking into your performance space or when speaking, you will likely not be in Stature and you may have forgotten to breathe. Remember, Stature is not simply standing up straight or standing at attention. It is embodying your Persona—the integral commitment to be yourself expressed through your body language. When you notice, stop, and *pull the thread*, putting yourself in Stature, *allow*—do not take—a breath, and begin again. Then, review what you have done. As you have already discovered when you are in Stature and breathing effectively, your voice is stronger. As you have previously begun to recognize, you are more confident and grounded. Now let's begin to enhance and refine these basic principles.

Fine-Tuning the Message

Always remember your goal is sovereignty—"supreme excellence or an example of it." *Everything matters.* At the conclusion of a two-and-a-half-hour session I recently had with Jeff, a senior executive of an international consulting firm, I provided a summary of that day's consultation. The meeting had focused on the most significant presentation of his career to be delivered three weeks from our lesson date. The previous week, Jeff had been given high marks by a senior partner who had critiqued his PowerPoint and Q&A rehearsal. She actually rated him 10 out of 10 on her scale, but he privately knew that on the "Arthur scale," as he called it, he might not rate so high. The stakes were very high. The successful outcome of this latest initiative would represent several hundred millions of dollars in new business to the corporation and a hefty bonus for him. My parting remarks that day were to practice visually, connect and be Consciously Aware of everything he did, and not to rush through the details.

I laid out the following short-term routine to follow. Just as you have been learning, each time he practiced, he was asked to practice either on video or in the mirror with an audio recorder and walk into his "performance space" in Stature. Even before doing that, while standing in the wings, he was to mentally catalogue the Vocal Awareness Rituals and notice every detail—from breathing to the release of tongue, jaw, neck, and shoulder tension to what happens when he notices himself successfully in Stature and his chest opens and his eyes become brighter.

I instructed him to not rush while walking in. His stride and walking speed had to represent his Persona/Brand. Once he hit his mark, I told him to not habitually blurt out "Good afternoon, my name is . . ." and launch into his presentation. Instead, upon hitting his mark, he was to take no more than five seconds to center himself, employ his CLB, and begin. While continuing to practice, he was to notice the resting place of his hands with his arms relaxed and fingers laced in front of him.

Always remember *everything matters.*

He was reminded not to stage his gestures, but to let them be *naturally congruent and purposeful*. His gestures must be strong and definitive when necessary, warm and expansive when appropriate, and never repetitive. He was developing his visual acuity. In doing so, he was learning to be mindful of everything he did, including *seeing* the pictures of his narrative in his mind's eye. At one point to practice storytelling, we had videotaped recordings of his reading fairytales to his young son. Upon viewing, he was fascinated to discover that when he was reading to his son, the expression in his voice, on his countenance, and most especially in his eyes was immediately connected to what he was saying. He also observed that what he read was more expressive, and how he said it, more earnest and compelling.

When reviewing his daily practice, Jeff was also encouraged to be critically discerning—to notice as many details of his performance as possible and where appropriate *self correct*.

As his preparation got under way, his integral commitment to excellence (not perfection) was, to the best of his ability, sacrosanct. Even the most mundane details, such as consciously carrying himself in Stature and not rushing his opening greeting, were practiced over and over. Jeff was mystified at how many times he had to begin again. He noticed subtle flaws and unconscious behaviors he had previously been unaware of—from his eyes darting around the room to his tongue and jaw tension which made him appear anxious and less poised. He had been a successful business leader for 15 years, had made hundreds of PowerPoint and other presentations. Frankly, until discovering Vocal Awareness, he had never realized how average his presentations were. He was now committed to the Vocal Awareness concept of the *Bottom Line* and *raising his personal bar*.

A strategic point must be made here. As Jeff began to conscientiously integrate all of his Vocal Awareness tools into his daily Communication Mastery regimen, instead of the process becoming laborious and the results forced, he actually noticed his *Conscious Awareness* peaking and his performance uncannily more natural and effective. Albeit a quixotic insight, it was a transformational moment. With this recognition, his ability to be a substantially more effective communicator took a quantum leap.

Jeff was also a committed recreational athlete. Through the years of his athletic training, he had observed that, when he mastered a skill set, this in turn enhanced the efficiency of his running, cycling, and so on. Not only did his body work more efficiently, but mind/body integration was more consistently present. When training or competing, he *saw with his mind's eye* what he needed to do. This enabled him to perform better, and the connection was critical for him. In developing Communication Mastery, the same training principles were in place and the same mind/body integration occurred. It was then that he remembered an axiom from our first session, *Mastery is Mastery*.

Building Blocks—Core

Everything in Vocal Awareness is connected to our core. Our core values and principles reflect the integrity and authenticity of who we are. They let people know what we stand for. They inform everything about us—our behaviors, our actions, the decisions we make, and the trust others place in us. Core is the infrastructure of responsible leadership. Of course, core has many other meanings and interpretations. Adjectives such as key, basic, essential, fundamental, principal, and vital, and nouns such as basis, essence, nucleus, and quintessence come to mind. However, the application of the word and concept of core will now focus on core as the fulcrum, the exact physical point for everything you do in Communication Mastery. It impacts Stature from the sound of your voice to your physical presence—the confidence you exhibit—the very essence of how you convey yourself requires a consummate connection to core at all times. Your understanding and effective use of this foundational piece will impact everything you do. Physically, spiritually, and emotionally, *core means support.* When you use your abdominal muscles to project your voice and when you commit to the Work, you support yourself.

Over the last generation, from yoga to Pilates to daily gym workouts, core strength has been emphasized. Certainly it has been paramount for athletes and dancers since time immemorial. In athletics and dance, core is a prerequisite for balance and power. A strong core also helps prevent injury, helps strengthen our lower back, and so much more. Finally, the importance and necessity of developing strong core muscles has filtered down to the rest of us.

Earlier I stated that Vocal Awareness is a *being* Work, but that we have to *do* to *be.* I have also said that *nothing in this work is linear, it is always integrative.* Nowhere is it more important to understand the intersection of these two maxims than when they coalesce in our practice and implementation of the Core Principle. Core work is physical work. It is mental work especially in the beginning as we must remember to engage our core (abdominal) muscles to effectively do everything we seek to accomplish in Communication Mastery. It is spiritual work. Standing and projecting from core, physically and energetically, is essential for embodying your Persona Statement and fulfilling your vision for yourself. When you see yourself in the mirror and hear yourself recorded, you quickly recognize that, when communicating from core, everything you do and say is more effective.

Physically, core is three inches below your navel. While placing your hand on your stomach just below your navel, please take a moment to contract your stomach muscles inward. Now release. While keeping your hand in place, contract your stomach muscles again but this time *up and in*. Notice that the pull comes from below your beltline. This critical distinction will enhance everything you do in Communication Mastery and is the foundation for your vocal support.

Without overstating it, core is intrinsic to the Vocal Awareness/Communication Mastery understanding of the term "life support."

Core Support

One of the original definitions for the word *support* combines the phrase *supportare* in Latin meaning "from below" with *portare* meaning "to carry." When we support our voice *from 3 inches below* our navel, it effectively *carries* and connects our sound and our energy in everything we say and do. Support is also a metaphor for *being there for ourselves*. As stated earlier, when engaging this principle of core and support effectively, you will produce a vocal sound that may momentarily intimidate you with its vocal strength, vitality, and the physical freedom you experience. This vocal and personal liberation is exactly the point of the Work. Remember Tony Robbins's interpretation of the Vocal Awareness Rituals/Checklist as "pattern interrupts." When we practice supporting our sound in the manner described above by *pulling up and in*, we are interrupting an old pattern which is not to support our voice and thus speak from the neck up. The old pattern is supplanted with a new one that dynamically represents all of who we are.

Exercise: "The Vertical Sit-Up" helps you become aware of how to engage your core and coordinate it through your voice. Stand in Stature and contract your abdominal muscles *up and in* for five repetitions. Please remember not to rush, and to begin each set of five with a *conscious, loving breath (CLB)*. Note: this muscle contraction exercise is designed to only work your abdominal muscles and coordinate your thought process enabling you to send your voice soaring through the Edge and Arc. You will notice, however, your habit may be to also tighten your neck and shoulders while learning this exercise. Please do not engage any other part of your body except your core muscles. *Mastery = mindfulness.*

Once you feel confident that you are doing this exercise correctly, please consistently integrate it into your daily Vocal Awareness Workout. Practice core/support in your walk, in your presentation, while sitting, and consciously integrate it into your professional life. You will discover immediate benefits.

Eye Contact

We all know the adage, *the eyes are the window to the soul*. In Vocal Awareness we add, *the voice is the window opened up*. Communication Mastery requires we employ every tool in our tool kit to maximize strategic opportunity. Like our voice, our eyes, convey everything about who we are, albeit subliminally—a message is always being sent. Eye contact *connects* us—literally and figuratively— with one another. Making eye contact changes the sound of your voice. You may notice a subtle shift in pitch—lower, enhanced resonance and vocal energy. When we avoid eye contact, our communication will lack warmth, be less expressive, and people may also interpret fear, anxiety, and rudeness. When we look one another in the eye, our listener gleans confidence, integrity, and authenticity from us. In addition, our voice/communication is experienced as more genuine.

Practice integrating this additional awareness while looking at yourself in the mirror delivering a fundamental moment of your prepared statement. First embody the phrase to the best of your abil-ity as you have been to this point. Next, practice while being mindful of using your eyes to visually connect to the import of your message. Your eyes may expand, your brows, knit or raise. They may "com-ment" as you consciously connect your eyes to the Vocal Awareness annotation incorporated in your text. Please remember to record yourself and listen back. Using your eyes strategically impacts your vocal and visual expression in every way—greater dynamic range, more compelling storytelling, and enhanced authenticity.

Another way to practice eye contact is to focus your attention on a specific area in the room and speak directly to it. Initially your eyes may flutter or you may feel a bit self-conscious. However, stick with it. This exercise will enhance your visual and mental focus and overall communication stamina—enabling you to embody the 6th Ritual of Vocal Awareness—Pay Attention/Deeper Listening—while effectively organizing your thoughts and staying on message.

Making eye contact when speaking can be difficult. We are so-ciologically conditioned to look at one another while the other is doing the speaking and we are listening. However, when we begin to speak, some of us habitually look away to *gather a thought*. Subliminally, what may be the catalyst for averting your eyes may also be discomfort with owning your message, or your fear of being too direct or intrusive. Avoiding eye contact is another example of the Vocal Awareness principle of the two greatest fears—*claiming your power* and *fear of abandonment*.

Your ability to claim each moment can literally be acquired in a matter of minutes. What may have seemed intractable is actually not. As you begin to acquire this critical new skill, you may be astonished to discover how many times you look away or your eyes avert your listener's eyes. Each time you notice, simply stop and begin again. You may be surprised at how many times you look away. You will be equally amazed at how quickly this lifelong habit disappears.

Gestures

As we've already spoken to some degree about gestures, here are a couple of additional tactical observations.

Gestures must always be genuine. They should never be forced, repetitive, or predictable. Instead, they should be natural, authentic, and *spontaneous*.

In Communication Mastery, everything must be integrated and part of the whole. Effective gestures can make a positive contribution but can just as easily take away from the desired effect. To practice, first stand comfortably in front of the mirror or camera, centering yourself with your Vocal Awareness Checklist visible. Again, using your prepared remarks as a template, initially deliver your opening or closing for one minute with your hands hanging comfortably at your side or *laced* in front of you. Using *no* gestures, simply try to relax and communicate your message. The second time through, beginning in the same Consciously Aware manner, add gestures as seem appropriate. If recording, please review and repeat until you are comfortable with your *performance*.

Telephone Communication— Integrating the Work

You have already heard me say numerous times in this book, *the same person shows up everywhere*. Speaking on the telephone is no different and is as important to your business success as a keynote address or a crucial PowerPoint presentation. Your new commitment to communication excellence stipulates that you can *never be on automatic pilot*. Everytime airline pilots climb into the cockpit, they have their checklist and redundancies, and never leave out one element of their preflight routine.

In this regard, *prior to every business phone call*, keep the Vocal Awareness Checklist in your direct line of sight. This will not only help your mental focus, but also enhance your visual focus, enabling you to sound more alert and attentive during the conversation. As in every other facet of this Work, speaking on the telephone is another way to embody the message and the messenger. In Communication Mastery the adage *business as usual* no longer applies.

Awareness of your Persona—your brand—frames everything. A summary of reminders for effective phone conversation begins with Stature. As always, when in Stature, do not let your head dip or lift. Maintain it at a perpendicular angle. This is particularly important on the telephone as lowering or raising your head negatively impacts your vocal energy and optimal pitch. Next, as you speak, combine Stature with Support remembering to pull your abdominal muscles *up and through the sound*. Always employ visceral language to the best of your ability. Strive to see everything you say in your mind's eye. In critical conversations, I even recommend jotting down key bullets and annotating them in Visceral Language. This will strategically enhance your impact during the conversation. Communicate from the *hub of your voice*—remember this is your core sound. Do the "finding the hub . . ." exercise before getting into the office in the morning or immediately before critical calls. It can be done very quietly and never needs to be disruptive or obvious. Eye contact: mentally envision the person you are speaking with. Engage effective storytelling by using an appropriate tempo along with changes of pace when necessary. Body language and gestures communicate on the telephone—be judicious.

In Vocal Awareness, as you know, the goal is *to always be our authentic self*. Nowhere is that more important than when speaking on the phone. Your unconscious behavior is to not project vocally or energetically. Therefore, you habitually may remain "a data delivery machine." When in Conscious Awareness, you always create the opportunity to cogently and persuasively convey your message. (Whenever necessary, refer back to earlier chapters and Appendix I to refresh the basics.)

Before initiating a call, take a moment to focus on the goal of your call. In addition, write out an opening and closing paragraph with accompanying bullets just as you have learned to do for your PowerPoint presentation. If someone calls you, whenever possible, have your Vocal Awareness Checklist nearby to focus you and your response. In this day of cell phones and walking down the street or driving in the car engaged in business conversations, you are multitasking and can easily be distracted from the primary focus of the call. Therefore, it is critical that the protocols you are learning be intentionally embedded in your communication DNA. Conscious Awareness is your *new normal*. There is no *on/off switch*.

Context Does Not Determine Outcome

For decades, I have been privileged to teach the best and the brightest—from the boardroom to the playing fields of virtually every major sport, I have taught men and women who aspire to excellence. In first lessons, I often create a role play for them.

For example, a few years ago I was teaching a man who is considered by many to be the greatest basketball player in the history of the sport. I asked him to visualize himself on the court at the free-throw line and go through his rituals and, then, shoot a free-throw. When he completed it, I asked him to step away from the free-throw line and I established a new image for him to see. I said: "The elbow on your shooting arm is inflamed and very painful. The foul you are shooting was caused by an aggressive player who knocked you to the floor and your head bounced off the surface. Thus, you are still a bit dizzy as you come to the line. You are in the opposing team's arena and it's a championship game where everything is on the line. For the first time in your life, you do not feel as confident as you would like to feel as you step up to shoot another free-throw. When you can envision the moment, go through your rituals again, then proceed to shoot the free-throw."

When he completed the second role play, I asked him once more to step away from the free-throw line and I changed the imagery a third time. I said: "Physically, everything is the same as in the second exercise. The only difference is that I want you to resume being the supremely confident man and extraordinary athlete you are. When you are ready, please step back to the free-throw line and shoot." Everything changed! I then asked him, "Did I ask you to behave differently from one scenario to the other?" He said, "No." Continuing, I said: "I changed the scenario. You changed the behavior. In the first example, you *went through the motions*. In the second, your breathing was tighter, your body a bit tense. In the third one, everything was in balance, focused, even the intensity in your eyes changed." I summarized the exercise in this way: *"The way we think and feel about something changes the way it is.* I changed the scenario, you changed the behavior. The lesson to be learned here is: The same person shows up everywhere. *Context does not determine outcome."*

Another time, I explored the same principle with an Olympic Gold Medal soccer player. She was also cocaptain of her victorious World Cup team. We did three different versions of her defending a penalty kick. Again, everything changed in the third scenario including taking more time with her prekick rituals.

The third example is a public-speaking role play with one of the most high profile attorneys in America. He is "the deal maker"—always behind the scenes. We had already been working together for a few years when he was required to give what was perhaps the most important public interview of his life. Interestingly enough, this was the first interview he had granted on television. Personally, he is private if not a bit shy. In a negotiation, he is dynamic and carries an attitude of invincibility. The role play we went through was based on his recall of an event in his life a number of years earlier when he was in his mid-twenties. I asked him to remember what it was like to be a young attorney walking into a meeting with a potential client who was, to date, the most prestigious individual he had ever been asked to possibly represent. In the first iteration, he walked in as himself—comfortable and relaxed. In the second, when I asked him to feel less confident and somewhat in awe of the person he was about to meet, he became more tentative—his arms stiffened as he walked, his stride shortened, and his pitch was higher when he introduced himself. In the final version, I asked him to embody his Vocal Awareness Persona and envision an affirmative outcome before proceeding—at which point he put himself in Stature and breathed. When walking into the room, his stride elongated and his visage changed. When he spoke, his voice was warm and confident, the pitch was lower, and his vocal energy stronger.

When the day of his televised interview arrived, I was sitting with him in the green room at the studio. Before he walked out, I reminded him, "Please remember, we are not our behaviors. Em-

body whom you choose to be. You are extraordinary—claim it."
Because he was so compelling, what had originally been scheduled
as a 10-minute question-and-answer segment stretched to 45 minutes. Even though that was his first on-air interview, no one knew
for he appeared completely at ease.

Earlier you will recall my saying, "We only want people to
know what we want them to know." The preceding stories are
profound real-life examples of transformative experiences that do
not only change a moment but impact a life.

Whether I do this exercise with ballet dancers, "weekend war-
riors," or politicians, whatever the role play, each example touches
something within the person doing the role play, and their performance changes. It may be subtle or obvious. At no time are they
identical. What is uncovered is something basic to the human condition, yet previously not understood. *Each and every one of us must
choose who shows up when challenged with adversity or confronted by an
extraordinarily positive, potentially life-changing moment.*

Take a moment and experience this exercise for yourself.
Identify an event you would like to role play. Please notice as
much as possible the intellectual, emotional, and/or physical shifts
and adjustments you make, or your mind/body/spirit system intuits. When you complete it, please jot down your discoveries in
your Vocal Awareness journal so that at any time you may go back
to your notes and reflect. Without overstating it, it is imperative
to recognize the role unconscious behaviors play in every critical,
decision-making moment of your life—professionally or personally. Such behaviors can either vanquish you or help you excel
and fulfill your vision. When you understand that *context does not
need to determine outcome*, you understand that *the choice is yours*.
You can then create the opportunity to achieve excellence in
everything you do.

Adding the Final Elements: The Art of the Interview

A successful interview in any format or situation—from job to media interviews—is framed by the Boy Scout motto: "Be Prepared." Whether you are conducting the interview or being interviewed, everything you are learning in this book applies. I teach these skills to every client. The interview format is always the same, regardless if I am working with a novice or the most seasoned professional—physicians, journalists, attorneys, CEOs, CFOs, headhunters, HR directors, athletes, artists, or college students. First, "Be Prepared" means to know as much as you can about the subject matter and the person/organization you are interviewing or who is interviewing you. Be clear about the purpose and/or goal of the interview. Each time you practice, practice in Vocal Awareness. Always begin with a clear understanding of your Persona/Brand and reference your Checklist as necessary. Always work in front of the mirror and with your camera or audio recorder on. Write out and annotate a few questions and answers using the same format discussed in Chapter 4. You will benefit from this mental/visual interface. In addition, remember: "Less is more." The questions and answers you craft should be concise. They can be complex but not complicated. This is a comprehensive discipline that will enhance communication clarity.

If possible, role play and record a hypothetical interview with a partner. Each time you review your *game film*, please be as objective and discerning as possible in order to ensure that each subsequent practice benefits from your keen observations. In each practice, please challenge yourself to incorporate the many techniques and insights you are learning. Recall the Vocal Awareness adage, "Don't leave pieces out." From premeeting rituals to walking into the room and standing or sitting during the interview, your body language, gestures, eye contact, the pitch of your voice, breathing technique, and sincerity all matter.

Lastly, a critical but often overlooked skill is to train yourself to be an excellent listener—internally and externally. This skill is as important to an interview as is the preparation for the interview. As you develop the ability to listen internally, monitoring any emotional static—such as, self-judgment, doubt, and anxiety (examples of "white noise" which may disrupt your concentration and *performance*), practice listening to the person you are speaking with. *When we auditorially engage, we are visually engaged*—from enhanced eye contact to relaxed and natural body language. It is an art form to be able to genuinely listen and hear the myriad nuances in a given conversation. The flow of the narrative between ourselves and our conversation partner—grammar, syntax, and intelligence—is both a critical business practice and strategic personal opportunity. *It is a performance, but we don't want to see the performance. We want to see you.*

A Few Remaining Performance Tips

We only want our audience to know what we want them to know.

➤ For any public meeting—from PowerPoint to keynote address—build rehearsal time actually in the meeting space into your schedule. Even if you only have a few minutes before your audience arrives, you will derive benefits from recording and listening back as well as familiarizing yourself with the environment (i.e., sightlines, acoustics, and so forth).

➤ Whether an interview or public address, practice everything as you prepare! There is no aspect that is too mundane—you want to minimize surprises. Practice when to look down and when to look up; practice page turns; practice how you sit and walk.

➤ In a large space or when speaking from a podium, even if there is a podium microphone, a lavaliere microphone is always preferable. Speaking into a podium mic can negatively affect the angle of your head and does not let you visually relate to your audience as a lavaliere does. A lavaliere mic also affords you the freedom to move about and gesture when appropriate. It is always best to arrange for a lavaliere mic ahead of time. When there is a contract, state the request in writing, as some facilities may have to rent one.

➤ Whenever possible, have your notes or script preset. Whether you prefer note cards or a binder, walking in with your hands free is more polished and professional than having something in your hand or inside a jacket pocket.

➤ It is helpful to have room temperature water available to sip, either on the table in front of you in a conference room or on the under shelf of a podium. Not only is water necessary once in a while to clear your throat, but if you build "sipping moments" into your notes and/or script, it also creates an opportunity to pause and gather yourself and refocus.

➤ Grooming and attire—think of what you wear as your performance uniform or wardrobe. How you dress reflects your brand. Your hairstyle, makeup, every detail speak volumes. The last thing to do before walking on stage or going into the meeting is to use the mirror to confirm that your appearance is as you want it to be.

➤ The last minute—once you are ready, use this minute to focus on yourself, your Persona, your Stature, your Goals. No distractions. This is your moment.

Practice Makes Excellence

To aspire to excellence requires that we surrender—to serve our Call, our Goals, our highest aspirations. Equally important, striving for excellence allows for "mistakes," which are requisite building blocks for self-development.

Quoting two of the greatest men of the twentieth century on the subject of mistakes, Albert Einstein said, "Anyone who has never made a mistake has never tried anything new." Winston Churchill said, "All men make mistakes, but only wise men learn from their mistakes."

The practice of Communication Mastery requires a commitment not to perfection, but to excellence, and never considers mistakes errors, but opportunities to discover and learn. Striving for perfection actually inhibits us. Being "perfect" traps us in a quagmire of repressed expectations. The basic theme is: "I can never be perfect enough, so why try?" When we do not try, we do not risk. *Without risk there is no growth.* The desire for self-betterment is primal. It is in our very essence to conquer our circumstance and improve our lives. When we do not strive to enhance ourselves or our situation, it is as though we are in stasis—neither moving forward nor backward.

A commitment to excellence is a commitment to your Self. Fear, doubt, and self-judgment are synonyms for self-destruction. They not only impede your professional success, they inhibit your personal success and perpetuate mediocrity. To do this Work at the level of excellence you seek and deserve requires a belief system that says *nothing will stop me and I will never again stop myself.*

Action Step ··········▶

Create a one-month commitment to consistently work in front of a mirror with audio or video replay available. If there is an opportunity to have a legitimate short-term business goal (i.e., a forthcoming presentation or interview), this would be an excellent project. If there is nothing on your immediate horizon, please create a relevant business presentation to practice. You can use this opportunity to practice embodying your Mission or Vision Statement, or the opening/closing paragraph from a professional sales call. Your one-month project might also anticipate any significant address, interview, or future presentation.

The segments you initially practice should not be longer than two minutes. As you achieve success with the first two minutes, you will progress with each successive two minutes, and ultimately the entire presentation or interview preparation becomes exceedingly easier, more natural, and more effectively delivered.

In Communication Mastery the emphasis is always on *mastery*. This is the reason each practice is so specifically targeted. Not only are you learning new skills, you are discarding old habits. Attention to detail, repetition, and Conscious Awareness are the order of the day. You have begun to discover how much work it takes to *be yourself* in public or on camera. The result of your dedicated practice will be evident in the ease and authenticity of your message and the impact you, as the messenger, have on others.

7

THE HUMAN ACHIEVEMENT MOVEMENT: FULFILLING THE JOURNEY

There is a human striving for self-transcendence. It's part of what makes us human. With all of our flaws, we want to go a little bit further than we've gone before and maybe even further than anyone else has gone before.

—George Leonard

The origin of the word *potential* comes from Middle English. The Latin root, *potentialis* means "power" and *potent*, means *being able*—in other words being able to achieve power. The adjectival definition of *potential* is "having or showing the *capacity* to develop into something *in the future*." The Middle English origin of the word *achieve* means to "complete successfully." From Old French *achever* is "come" or "bring to a head." The interpretation of the noun *achievement* states "a thing done successfully, typically by effort, courage, or skill." *To achieve something is to accomplish it.*

In 1965, George Leonard created the term "Human Potential Movement." Two generations later, Vocal Awareness reframes the concept as the "Human Achievement Movement." Implicit to our understanding of the Human Achievement Movement is the recognition that, as we dedicate ourselves to fulfilling our vision and mastering the requisite skills, we manifest the ability to achieve what we seek. To sustain and excel requires the courage and tenacity to do what it takes to achieve our goal. What may only have been perceived as potential now becomes reality.

The Macro View: Communication Strategy and Integrative Leadership

The Human Achievement Movement compels us to identify with and claim our highest ideals—one of which is the betterment of society. When this is accomplished, we all prosper—*prosperity/success is the foundational bottom line of all business.*

> *In Communication Mastery your understanding of the "bottom line" must also include the way we speak with one another. It is not only the way we speak, but the way we relate and interact. It is imperative we not communicate stereotypically or behave territorially. As we transform ourselves, we transform society. Historically, the prevailing notion has been that words and language define us. Through Vocal Awareness you are clearly learning that perspective is limited. Instead your new understanding is* not only language defines us, but the way we deliver the message and embody the messenger are imperative.

In 1997, social psychologist Martin Chemers described leadership as "a process of social influence in which one person can enlist the aid and support of others in the accomplishment of a common task."[1] Through the integrative principles of Vocal Awareness and Communication Mastery, the goals of the Human Achievement Movement can be attained—true leadership in which each of us both interpersonally and intrapersonally embody and communicate our highest ideals with integrity and respect. When this is accomplished, you will have metamorphosed and created a new paradigm: prosperity and success are not only the foundational bottom line of business, but also of life.

You now empirically recognize that *your voice is not simply your mind out loud, and it is not only what you say but how you say it that matters.* You have also learned that it is no longer necessary or acceptable to speak without Conscious Awareness. With this knowledge and ability, you can take the next steps in your journey to Communication Mastery—becoming a Communication Strategist. With this new perspective and ability you can inspire, energize, and ultimately lead change within yourself and your organization.

No communication is simply external (i.e., only directed outwardly to our listener) but, simultaneously, is always connected internally. We may not hear it or even be aware of it, but, energetically, the internal conversation exists. *While connecting to and speaking with others and striving to serve their needs, we serve our own.*

Within this context, it is now essential to address the age-old question, "What's in it for me?" Your audience—whether yourself, an employee, a shareholder, or the public; one, thousands, or millions—is always asking consciously or subliminally this very same question. Last spring, I attended a corporate symposium and listened to three global titans in a panel discussion—CEOs from the entertainment, food, and media industries. The consistent message: corporate success is achieved by addressing the above question through customer satisfaction, establishing personal connection, and fulfilling emotional satisfaction. For a company to succeed, it must be open to change—to constantly evaluate and evolve. To this, Vocal Awareness adds we, too, must evolve. It is equally imperative to be recognized as a trustworthy leader— knowledgeable, caring, and integrating attributes such as integrity, intelligence, and passion.

Martin Buber, one of the most important philosophers of the twentieth century, established a philosophy of personal dialogue that reflects reality and human existence through the prism of integration. He called it "I and Thou." In other words, man's basic nature is to be in simultaneous relationship with ourselves, one another, and a higher consciousness at all times. Our dialogue and connection with each other is always harmonious and interdependent. Even in opposition, harmony may be dissonance, but we are connected. *Nothing is unrelated or exists in a vacuum or in isolation. We are always interrelated and interdependent.* On the one hand, "I/thou" is a complex but paradoxically simple interpretation illustrating that *Communication is always both intrapersonal and interpersonal. When we serve our audience, we serve ourselves and vice versa.*

With Martin Buber's prescient insights, "What's in it for me?" is never self-serving or territorial but is always seen through the lens of wholeness and commitment to the greater good. Buber had also stated:

> *There are three principles in a man's being and life, the principle of thought, the principle of speech, and the principle of action. The origin of all conflict between me and my fellow-men is that I do not say what I mean and I don't do what I say.*[2]

The ethical foundation of Communication Mastery—to be in mind/body/spirit consciousness embodying the integrity of who we are—resolves this conflict.

The Micro View: Communication Strategy/Integrative Leadership

The emphasis of Integrative Leadership and a prerequisite for fulfilling our journey is to be in service to the Work to the best of our ability, whether subliminally or through direct action. The following three sections will enhance your understanding, your vision and, also, serve as a Vocal Awareness practicum for your daily life.

The Five Pillars of the Work

The Five Pillars will help you stay the course and sustain your resolve enabling you to fulfill all you set out to achieve. Use this matrix regularly as your moral barometer, your ethical compass.

Consciousness means to become fully aware of everything you do, to the best of your ability. Remember that commitment to excellence requires an integrative approach. You should be attentive to your daily Vocal Awareness Workout and maintain a conscientious, dedicated, and respectful allegiance to the skill sets required for Communication Mastery as you consistently strive to not only *do* your best, but to *be* your best.

Vision refers to clearly seeing what you want to achieve then diligently committing yourself to doing whatever it takes in a respectful and professional manner to fulfill your Vision.

Integrity is your reputation—the moral fiber of who you are and how you want to be known. The commitment to embody your Persona, Mission, Vision, and Goals Statements in everything you do is fundamental to this principle.

Integration and Integrity share the same root source—wholeness. Everything is integrative: mind/body/spirit; practice/application; goals/timeline; breath/voice; and so on. Integration is

the transformational turning point in Communication Mastery—
nothing exists in isolation.

Mastery is a noble pursuit—a life-long dedication to excellence—an adherence to a set of guidelines that requires us to be our
best. Mastery is sovereignty.

Strategic Insights

Over the course of a lesson or seminar, I always "check in" with
students/clients with queries such as: Do you understand? Does
this make sense? Do you have any questions you want to ask or
statements you wish to make? This teaching style creates an opportunity to both engage with the student/client while, at the
same time, encouraging them to take a moment and consciously
reflect within themselves. As you manifest your ability to claim and
embody Communication Mastery, employ the same dialectic with
yourself: Do I understand? Am I just going through the motions or
am I truly paying attention? Do I believe in myself? This technique
of checking in is an important learning tip. It is a way to be more
fully in Conscious Awareness.

This moment also creates an opportunity to introduce a new
concept essential to the boldness of your new undertaking: the distinction between assumption and presumption. For example, even
if you think you empirically understand a particular technique that
you have learned what you need to know and may move on, please
never assume this to be true. Never assume that you fully compre-
hend what is being said in this chapter but *presume* that you have
the ability to fulfill its goals.

Another take on the concept of assumption/presumption is: in
any presentation, never *assume* that you need time to get to know
your audience, or they you. There is no time. Remember: an opinion is created in three seconds, and *the meeting begins before you walk*

into the room. Also, in any presentation never *assume* that you have got it down and can go on "automatic pilot." That is a recipe for disaster. You will no longer be attuned to where you are or where you are going. Invariably, you will *go unconscious*, stop listening to yourself, and revert to old behaviors.

A third interpretation refers to a precept introduced in Chapter 2: "The Two Greatest Fears"—fear of abandonment and fear of claiming our own greatness, ownership of our power. It is imperative to this discussion that you deeply grasp how the notion of assumption is often insidiously woven into the very essence of how we communicate (i.e., in business we often *assume a role*). In doing so, we may subsume ourselves and, unbeknownst to us, our coworkers may perceive us as superficial, timid, or inauthentic. Ownership requires initiative. In business and in life *presume* you have the right to be who you are. This is a core tenet of Communication Mastery.

Surrender/Serve/Soar

About 15 years ago, I was at Palm Sunday Mass with my wife. As I was reflecting during the service, what emerged was the mantra "serve/soar/surrender." These three words immediately became part of my daily meditative and spiritual rituals. A few years later during the High Holydays I experienced a profound revelation. I had the order wrong. It is not serve/soar/surrender rather it is *surrender/serve/soar*. This epiphany condensed years of work, study, and focus into an elegant virtual haiku of Vocal Awareness. All we have to do is serve the Work.

Vocal Awareness/Communication Mastery is successful because it works. It works because it is based on decades of scientific, philosophical, artistic, and sociological research and practice. Equally important, it succeeds because I require myself to be accountable.

My students and clients have, in a manner of speaking, been the canvas on which I paint. However, I am the "lab rat" upon which all the work is first tested. Whatever I ask of my students, I have first asked of myself. The key to all this is to be *in service to the Work.*

I became a professional singer at 17. At one particular audition, as all the singers were in the waiting area warming up, pacing and practicing, I recognized I was intimidated by the "older men's voices"—older being the 25-year-olds. Their robust sound caused me to change my audition song to something less vocally dynamic and distinctive. When I didn't get the job, I thought about my actions and realized that it was my responsibility to be there for myself. No one could intimidate me unless I allowed them to. This is when the understanding of the principle "context does not determine outcome" began to emerge. It was at this same time the first seeds of Vocal Awareness were being planted. As I was developing as a singer, I was also becoming a fledgling teacher. I was 18 when I started working with my first student.

From the beginning of my artistic and professional journey, I have strived to be rigorous and as honest as possible. With this point of view, even from the outset, I looked at myself with an unvarnished eye and was forced to acknowledge my extreme lack of self-confidence and self-esteem. I often felt like the proverbial groundhog constantly darting back into my hole. I didn't have enough wherewithal to believe in myself. But an odd thing happened every time I performed. I could "show up for the Work," even though I couldn't show up for myself. Fortunately, I am a good listener, intrapersonally and interpersonally. Noticing this behavior led to the establishment of the first principles of Vocal Awareness. Among these first principles were the creation of a Persona Statement and the concept of Surrender—being in service to the Work. Once my Persona Statement was defined, little by little I began to gain confidence and clarity about how I wanted to be known, not just when I performed but at all times. Surrender provided the integral courage to show up, not just for the Work, but for my Self.

One of my students, a former football player, had an enormously successful National Football League career that included two Super Bowl wins. As we were working on CLB (Conscious, Loving Breath), he asked an intriguing question about the difference between taking a breath and allowing a breath. He felt the physiological energetic difference between *taking* and *allowing* but didn't understand why. He asked, "What do you mean by allow a breath?" I said, "Allowing a breath reconnects us with our primal state." I asked him to watch his infant son breathing while he slept, to gently place his hands on his rib cage and notice how his breathing was relaxed and expansive. I explained: "This intrinsic knowledge of breath remains in our energetic DNA so that when I ask you to allow a breath, you instinctively return to the same breathing pattern as your son—to breathe this way is your natural state and the body remembers."

Surrender/serve/soar are constant reminders to shift your behavior from habitual/unconscious to conscious/embodied. *In Communication Mastery, this is our primal state—Conscious Awareness in everything we do.*

Transformative Stories

To Achieve—We Must Leap

The humility to see things as they are and the audacity to believe you can make them different.

To achieve success and fulfill our goals is rarely easy. Oftentimes there can be significant adversity. When adversity strikes—and it may—know that you can overcome it and emerge stronger than before. It is like a grain of sand in an oyster shell. Adversity is necessary for success. Adversity creates the opportunity to rededicate, realign, and reemerge.

Akin to adversity is fear. We have all heard the axiom, "fear of failure." However, Vocal Awareness recognizes this understanding of fear as misappropriated. It is actually a *fear of excellence*. As the title of this section states: To achieve, we must leap. To leap, we must risk. The following is a personal story from my own journey—confronting my greatest fear/claiming myself.

By the age of 26 I had been teaching Vocal Awareness part-time for eight years. I had also worked many other full- and part-time jobs—singing, counseling, and teaching to name a few. Shortly after our first son was born, I was fired from my full-time job. Finances and life became very bleak. My wife and I even got to the point that we were on food stamps for several months. One night I was sitting alone in the living room of our first home when I was struck with the realization that I was afraid to teach Vocal Awareness full-time for fear that I would fail. The excuse had been my wife would not allow me to do so—that she wasn't there for me. This was a lie. She was there for me 1000 percent. In that moment, I was finally able to admit the truth—I was not there for myself. With that recognition, I was able to eradicate my fear. The next day, I placed an ad in a local college newspaper offering a free introductory Vocal Awareness lesson. One young woman called then who studied with me for many years and became a close personal friend. With this fledgling step, I embarked on the Vocal Awareness journey full-time. Within a couple of years, I had a burgeoning practice that included corporate and theatrical consultations, a private studio, and a firmly established Vocal Awareness matrix.

Over the years I have been privileged to interface with creative leaders from around the world. Their stories reflect the courage and commitment required to fulfill a vision. Leaders do not *play it safe. Leaders do whatever it takes to do and be their best.*

Cesar Millan, also known as the Dog Whisperer, is a former student of mine. He built a business empire based on his love of dogs. He once related a story of watching a pack of very large dogs walking down the street led by a Chihuahua not a Great Dane. The point was that the "big dog" (the Chihuahua) was the one who simply believed it was the leader and the other dogs followed. He said, *"Leaders don't run with the pack; they lead it."*

➤ ➤ ➤

In Chapter 5, I mentioned that I taught at Walt Disney Imagineering. Teaching there was a stunning opportunity to experience the interface between art and commerce firsthand. As I mentioned, I was initially brought in to help the artists and writers sell their creative proposals to the chairman, their management teams, and to sponsors. One of the first clients I taught there began working with me when he was in his mid-forties. Several years earlier, he had cancer and was so close to dying that he described seeing a "vortex." While crafting his vision statement during one of our sessions, I asked him about his background.

He had a degree in sculpting but no longer sculpted. When he completed his Mission Statement, it was to be a sculptor, but he had no portfolio of his work. For several weeks, I kept asking about his portfolio. He had made no progress. When I asked him why, he responded that he was afraid. I then asked, "What are you afraid of. You faced death. Everything else in life has to be a footnote." That got his attention. Within the next several months he sculpted for the first time in years. He completed his portfolio, entered a corporate competition, and won. His work—a large ornate fountain— became the centerpiece of a new hotel in Scottsdale, Arizona. He now sculpts full-time. Vocal Awareness reminds us of our responsibility and opportunity to be in service to our calling.

➤ ➤ ➤

Some time ago, I received an e-mail from the chairman of a multi-billion-dollar corporation I work with following a series of high-profile events at which he had spoken. The theme of our recent work had been Conscious Awareness and the technical trigger for enabling him to be in Conscious Awareness was the 3rd Ritual—Conscious, Loving Breath. In referencing the events where he spoke he opened the e-mail by saying, "I felt good . . ." The point here is he didn't speak about his voice, he spoke about himself. He knew that he sounded good and delivered well. What he recognized for the first time was that he *consciously and deliberately* embodied the message and the messenger. He was himself. He was not presenting himself. There was no artifice, nothing contrived, rather he embodied and revealed his authenticity.

➤ ➤ ➤

Recently, in two separate lessons with two distinctly different corporate leaders, one whose career path is finance and the other human resources, I virtually had the same conversation. I discussed their responsibility and opportunity as leaders in their respective organizations—to lead by example. I said:

> *Conscious Awareness is our goal, not just at work but in life. Whether in a personal or professional environment, when you actualize any one of the 7 Vocal Awareness Rituals, you trigger a paradigmatic shift from* business as usual—*unconscious, habitual behavior—to a more enlightened, astute, integral commitment to excellence. At this point everything changes. For example, vocally speaking, the pitch, timbre, vibrational energy of your voice is enhanced. At the same time, your ability to embody your highest aspirations for yourself is more successfully realized. In this state you are maximizing and achieving what is possible in the moment. You are fulfilling the Work.*

I continued by asking,

How often have you heard me say, "We cannot hold the space for another. We can only hold the space for ourselves."? When we serve ourselves, we serve our audience. It is not the other way around. Each time we serve ourselves, we confront and conquer our two greatest fears. Ultimately, we will eradicate *them, but this will occur over time.*

I reminded each of these fine women of three critical Vocal Awareness axioms: *Context does not determine outcome; the same person shows up everywhere; Vocal Awareness is not merely situational.* Once again, the point is that "Communication Mastery is life Work through the metaphor of Voice." I concluded each session by saying, "There is no greater opportunity to apply our learning and our ethical commitment to the Work than when we call upon ourselves to *show up* on our terms to the best of our ability each and every day." In this way we actually metamorphose behaviorally and energetically. Our internal compass is no longer fixed on *potential*, rather we respectfully recognize our *achievements*. This acknowledgment is critical—the recognition paramount. With this understanding we pass through a symbolic doorway *transitioning from settling for the status quo*, identifying with our potential, to actually *achieving what we have set out to accomplish*. This action requires courage and dedication. It changes our very belief system. The essence of how we project ourselves to others is altered. The earnest commitment to being our best is the ultimate act of surrender. *True service to who we are through what we do each and every moment of every day to the best of our ability ennobles not just ourselves but those we lead as well.*

➤ ➤ ➤

Earlier this year, I helped 12 high-profile business leaders, prepare for their annual meeting, including the chairman of the company. The Vocal Awareness theme from the chairman to his team was true service—the principles of ennobling and leadership. The team was directed to *embody not just the message, but the messenger.* Participants' job descriptions ranged from attorneys to executive vice presidents, department heads to division presidents. The chairman had been a longtime client of mine, and it was through his initiative that I shared Vocal Awareness with the team. They were all familiar with presenting at myriad corporate meetings and public events. However, the upcoming platform was the most significant opportunity any had had to formally present to all corporate stakeholders. This was also the first time any were required to read from a teleprompter. Presentation lengths ran from 4 to 10 minutes. We had three brief rehearsals.

From the first rehearsal to the final meeting, each individual did what a champion does to be successful—they worked exceedingly hard to embody the Work. They did Vocal Awareness warm-ups and paid meticulous attention to detail. This included recording rehearsals, private sessions with me, practicing Visceral Language annotation, and most important, observing the 3rd, 5th, 6th, and 7th Vocal Awareness Rituals. As you know, these specific Rituals address breathing, taking your time, paying attention, and being your Self.

At the conclusion, one of the participants wrote the following e-mail:

> *Your approach to assisting amateurs with public speaking is very interesting and clearly a learning experience for me. You are present in the beginning with your non-judgmental evaluation of all presentations, providing little clues to personal rather than group improvement. Public speaking is rarely pleasant or sought by most people. With your direction and assistance, everyone feels bet-*

ter about themselves, gains a littler personal pride, and the overall presentation improves greatly.

Following the event, one of the principal shareholders spotted me and stopped to share that the chairman's closing remarks were everything he had hoped they would be. He said he didn't simply experience the chairman's business acumen but was moved by his embodiment—his personal attributes and leadership excellence. Unbeknownst to the shareholder, the chairman's memorized remarks had been annotated and rehearsed in Visceral Language and were fully conveyed in Conscious Awareness.

As the chairman raised his own personal bar, by extension he raised the bar for the entire corporation. He always aspires to be his best and requires the same of everyone. His passion to be and to do inspires and drives himself and his team to fulfill their personal and corporate vision. The result is the commitment to dedicated achievement.

➤ ➤ ➤

To come to this point of *mastery* requires a significant amount of time practicing, recording, listening, observing, and refining. Repeat even the most "rudimentary" aspects of this Work, *consciously* and *conscientiously*. Focused, astute, disciplined practice and application are the ethos of a champion. *Through your respectful and diligent commitment to this mastery matrix, you are creating the foundation for your success.*

When asked, "Why do you teach?" a teacher may respond, "To make a difference." The following exemplifies an integral individual who is committed to excellence in everything she does.

Claudia is the comptroller for a multinational corporation based in Europe. She is the highest ranking woman in the organization. Her career path is to achieve CFO status with the company when the current CFO retires in five years. In addition to her responsibilities as comptroller, she spearheads the company's high-est profile public awareness campaign, which is designed to both enhance the public's knowledge of the company while at the same time helping to externalize the corporate mission. In preparation, approximately one year in advance of the rollout, she began study-ing with me. One of her goals, and an aspect of my responsibility, is for me to not only support her but also her team. She is often the conduit enabling men and women with entrenched positions to come together and communicate with one another for the good of the company. We have worked one-on-one in Europe, at seminars, and in regular Skype lessons.

One of the reasons Claudia was given this prestigious oppor-tunity was because of her consummate level of professionalism. Equally important is her ability to communicate, not simply as a business leader, but fully as herself. Her performance reviews have always reflected her trustworthiness and genuine nature, as well as what an excellent communicator she is.

We met at a Communication Mastery seminar I was teaching for the company. My initial observation of her was a unique blend of intelligence, insight, and sensitivity. I observed this through her interaction with colleagues, the nature of her questions, the imme-diacy of her implicit trust, and comprehension of the Vocal Aware-ness principles and exercises being taught.

At the close of the seminar, she asked to study with me. In our first lesson we focused on a principle she had learned in the semi-nar—*the same person shows up everywhere*. To support this concept she brought in her Persona, Mission, and Vision Statements which enabled us to create a synergistic map for her personal journey. Ear-lier I spoke about Claudia's innate ability. Part of my responsibility is to enable clients/students to understand the significance of their natural talent and, in turn, support them in effectively leveraging their talent in an integrative and strategic way. We all have a talent, some even have a gift. *Our responsibility is to integrate who we are into what we do.*

The next step was to help Claudia become more Consciously Aware—to begin to *hear herself* internally and externally as congruently as possible for the first time. The goal was to objectify and unify the uniqueness of who she was in as mindful a way as possible.

I asked her to record a few minutes of three different conversations for our next session—one in her professional capacity speaking with the CFO, one with a friend, and one with her teenaged son. In our subsequent Skype session, as I guided her listening, she played what she had recorded. She was astonished. Her business voice was fast, lacked expression, the pitch somewhat high. She described her listening experience by saying, "This woman is somewhat nondescript. She is merely conveying information and is not compelling to listen to."

In the second conversation with her friend, Claudia was speaking in her native tongue (English is her second language). Her first observation was, "I like this woman. She is warm and caring." I pointed out that her delivery was slower, there was more vitality in her sound, and the pitch of her voice was lower.

Speaking with her son was her favorite conversation to listen to. She immediately gasped when she heard it and said, "I can actually hear the love and warmth I feel for Kyle conveyed in my voice." I helped her recognize that, in this *version* of Claudia, the pitch of her voice was lower, and the intonation and expression the most authentic of the three. There was nothing artificial or forced.

I then explained why I asked her to make the three recordings. I told her:

> *What you just experienced was your old reality. Three different contexts; three different Claudias. You will recall in the work-shop the role play that illustrated* context does not deter-

mine outcome. *I would like your initial takeaway to be:* the same person shows up everywhere. *The three expressions we listened to are examples of how we each speak every day. At one level, they are simply normal conversations, and there is absolutely nothing wrong with them. However,* in Conscious Awareness, you have a choice as to how you want to be known. *That, in part, is the point of Communication Mastery. You are learning to choose. In a tactical business moment when what you want to say needs to be compelling and your audience riveted, you are now learning how to "tune in." Ultimately, you will never tune out. You will always be in the 6th Ritual—Pay Attention/Deeper Listening.*

Intrinsic to each of us is our unconscious need to individuate first ourselves, and then ourselves from others. In doing so, we label, categorize, and characterize: male/female; leader/follower; trustworthy/fraudulent; aggressive/compliant; intelligent/average; charismatic/uninteresting; strong/weak. We unconsciously, if not deliberately, project our points of view, and even our prejudices, onto one another. In a word we "judge."

Communication Mastery incorporates integration in a most complex and comprehensive way to create a new archetype designed to enable us to communicate intrapersonally and interpersonally as consciously and integratively as possible. This particular archetype asks us to see ourselves in the Gestalt of who we are. Traditionally, we stereotype, thus pigeonhole ourselves and one another. In doing so, our behavior prevents us individually and collectively from creating a society based on true equality and respect.

We must never *settle* for how things are, rather, *accept* how they are. Understanding, patience, dedication, and a steadfast commitment to excellence is always the goal.

Shifting the Paradigm:
A Call to Action

*Stimulated by those moods which poets turn into words, I turn my
ideas into tones which resound, roar, and rage until at last they stand
before me in the form of notes.*

—Ludwig van Beethoven[3]

Implicit in the paradigmatic shift, from striving to fulfill our potential to actualizing achievement, is a commitment to excellence
as well as a trust of and accountability to oneself. Please trust that
you actually have what it takes to accomplish what you set out to
achieve, and the accountability rests in the work ethic to complete
the required tasks.

A consummate example of human achievement is the story of
composer Ludwig van Beethoven. He was one of the most influ-
ential and renowned artists in history (1770–1827). Beethoven was
a revolutionary, not only in his music, but because of his ideas. The
ideas and musical motifs came easily but, by and large, integrating
the motifs into the whole to form a profound and unified piece of
music was exceedingly difficult. On occasion he was still changing
notes hours before he debuted a piece. He knew what he wanted
his music to say, but sometimes, saying it was difficult. He *heard* the
music in his head, but as he was deaf for most of his life, he could
not hear as others heard.

Beethoven did not exhibit the finest social graces. None of that
mattered to him. His entire life was dedicated to his art and, as an
astute businessman, also to commerce and his legacy. Beethoven
was a visionary. *His call to action was to do whatever it took to fulfill his
vision.* Because of his indefatigable determination, he established
a new paradigm in music. *He did not speak through his music so that*

others understood or agreed. He spoke through his art as he needed to. As a musician, he was supremely confident and self-aware. As a man, he was a tortured individual seeking to be understood.

In 1988, I was teaching in Vienna, Austria. While there, I toured Beethoven's home just outside of Vienna in the town of Heiligenstadt. Framed on a pedestal in the living room in front of the fireplace was a document referred to as the "Heiligenstadt Testament," written in 1802 to his brothers Johann and Karl. His will stipulated that it was not to be read until after his death. It is perhaps the most insightful, poignant, and revelatory letter I have ever read. Beethoven bears his soul, expressing his torment and desire to be understood, while at the same time, recognizing he may never be.

Ludwig van Beethoven is an example of the courage and dedication required to fulfill one's grand ambition without compromising our highest ideals. He was supremely dedicated to doing whatever it took to "turn [his] ideas into tones . . . until at last they [stood] before [him] in the form of notes."

Beethoven had a rare gift combined with a willingness to fulfill his art, including enduring loneliness and, on occasion, being perceived as a misanthrope. *His life is a consummate example of being in service to one's calling.*

When you know you have been called, you cannot simply hang up saying, "Sorry, wrong number." You must answer the call. Whether you are still defining your purpose or already doggedly pursuing it, through its meticulous structure Vocal Awareness will support your call to action. In the method, the seamless interface between you the individual and you the professional is always foremost. With the groundbreaking concept of "Spiritual Pragmatism" in Chapter 2, you are learning how to be yourself each moment, while at the same time strategically planning for your future. *The Work will always help you discover, define, redefine, and conscientiously dedicate yourself to what you envision.* To accomplish this requires shifting your own paradigm. Fundamental to this understanding may require a leap of faith. But, as I said earlier, "Always *know* even when you may not believe."

To be frank, many of us may not have a calling. We may not aspire to, or even conceptualize, making an extraordinary contribution. Instead we go through life doing our jobs, showing up every day to accomplish our assigned tasks. However, you are clearly not that individual. You aspire.

I was speaking with a client one day who is a senior HR executive for the largest and most successful corporation in her industry. We were discussing a leadership seminar I was going to give at her company three weeks later. In our 45-minute call, we were engaged in an open-ended conversation. She inquired of me: "Why do people speak as they do in business meetings, sometimes seeming distracted, lacking in vitality, speaking too rapidly? Sometimes critical detail is missing in their PowerPoint presentation either in their slides or verbal message as though they hadn't done their due diligence. This in turn makes it difficult for me to engage in a more complex and substantive conversation. To be honest, some, not all, are uninspiring."

My clear and succinct response was, "The word *average* is a word for a reason." At the conclusion of our discussion, I encouraged her to strive each day to ignite a spark within the employees in her organization and to never give up. I said: "They actually want to be their best, they simply don't know how. In the seminar you will teach them how to be better at their jobs. I will teach them how to be better at being themselves. Together we will drive change and ultimately, you will achieve the success you seek."

I closed the teleconference by reminding her of two Vocal Awareness axioms I introduced early in our collaboration: *Surrender—to be in service to the Work* and *One person can make a difference.*

"Both principles," I said, "remind us of the importance of being our best, and isn't that the point of the journey?"

Changing the World Through Voice

From its inception, this book was designed for you to arrive at this moment with the skills and understanding necessary for Communication Mastery. Whether the perspective has been business, technical, vocal/visceral/body language, philosophical, the anecdotes personal or professional, my goal has been to help illuminate your path. I also want to create an incandescent experience so compelling that it would be incomprehensible for you to choose to do anything other than fulfill your vision. To accomplish this, a combination of perseverance and a leap of faith are required. You must have an audacious, earnest, passionate, and consummate commitment to lead and to inspire your organization and yourself.

My mission is to Change the World Through Voice. It is my passion and commitment to do whatever it takes to the best of my ability to fulfill this Vision. But, I am obviously only one person. *Thus, the purpose and focus of this book has been to enlist you in the Human Achievement Movement—an opportunity to dedicate yourselves to excellence and to the fulfillment of your highest aspirations.* It is designed for you—leaders in business and those who aspire—to strategically manifest dynamic change in yourselves, your organizations, and/or your professions.

To achieve this reflects a dual responsibility. First, *my* responsibility is to teach clearly and effectively in order that you truly know how to "do the Work." From Stature to Conscious, Loving Breath, Edge and Arc to crafting your Persona Statement, preparing a PowerPoint presentation, rehearsing for a job interview, mobilizing your sales force, or consciously being your Self, Communication Mastery requires consummate technique. Second, *your* responsibility is to strive to be in the 6th Ritual of Vocal Awareness: Pay Attention/Deeper Listening.

In turn, please use this book to create a new paradigm for yourself and everyone you touch. Be like the rock that, when thrown into the pond doesn't merely make a splash and then sink to the bottom. Instead that splash, large or small, sends concentric rings across the pond impacting everything they come in contact with. Through this Work, just as the rings energetically extend across the surface of the pond, you, too, have the opportunity to make an impact. It is inevitable. Seize it! If one person can make a difference, imagine what millions together can do.

Action Step ··········➤

When you are finished reading this book, complete a game plan within one week. Use the protocols from this chapter to guide you in creating a realistic business/life strategy. Whether it is a spreadsheet or a handwritten document, it needs to be written to reflect and incorporate the principles and techniques you have acquired. Initially, break it down into weekly, monthly, and quarterly increments that cover one year. Please remember to include systematic review time as an aspect of your due diligence. This will enable you to not "overpromise and underdeliver." When you know your plan is succeeding, extrapolate it out to what, ultimately, will be a five-year plan.

Enjoy the journey!

AFTERWORD

The Work

For many years, I had the honor of teaching one of the great theologians and spiritual teachers of our time. We met while seated next to each other on a 12-hour flight from London to Los Angeles. We both recognized that it was as though our meeting had been preordained and had not happened simply by chance. During that flight, we learned that it was not our usual habit to engage fellow passengers in elaborate conversation. However, this trip was different. We couldn't refrain from speaking to one another. What emerged was a long and fruitful personal and professional relationship. Before he passed, we had become such good friends that he asked me to sing at his wedding.

When we met on that fateful flight, he was no longer a practicing minister; rather, he was the president of an international aid and relief organization. During one of our early sessions, he recounted a story of a trip through India with Mother Teresa. He shared: "As we walked along various byways from town to town, we saw so much poverty, so much death. There were a number of naked men and women lying by the side of the road, which prompted Mother Teresa and me to stop periodically at a local vendor's stall to buy a bolt of cloth to cover them. If there was shade nearby, we would carry them to the shaded area and gently place them there, covering them with a piece of the fabric we had purchased. If there was no shade, we would cover them where they lay, but there were so many. I realized in that moment, no matter how much we did, we could never do enough. There would always be more to do. In the same moment, I also recognized and accepted that each of us can only do as much as we are truly capable of doing. That is our allotment on this journey."

As you begin your Vocal Awareness journey, strive daily to fulfill your vision and sustain your commitment to your Self, to the work you do, and to your family and community. As my wise friend said, each of us can only do as much as we are truly capable of doing. That is our allotment on this journey. Be your best! Remember, we have the ability to make a difference!

APPENDICES

The root of the word *appendix* comes from the Latin *appendere* meaning to "hang upon." This section encapsulates virtually everything you have learned in this book. Use it often. It serves as a summary of key principles, axioms, meaningful quotations, techniques, and notable Vocal Awareness phrases including an acrostic on leadership that will further elucidate your understanding of the Work.

As you have discerned, I love language. In Appendix V titled "Leadership Terms: Definitions and Etymology," there is an opportunity to discover the origins of key words and concepts we use every day that are equally foundational to your embodiment of Communication Mastery.

APPENDIX I

The Work

Key Axioms

- Voice Is Power.
- The same person shows up everywhere.
- The two greatest fears: fear of abandonment and owner-ship of our power
- We are not our behaviors.
- Context does not determine outcome.
- Structure does not impinge, it liberates. Freedom without direction is chaos.
- Vocal Awareness is a *being* Work, but we have to *do* to *be*.
- An opinion is created in three seconds.
- It is not only the message but the messenger that matters.
- Do not be "the cork in your own bottle."
- A Champion does it differently.
- Our goal is excellence, not perfection.
- Critical to every communication is not only what we say, but how we say it.
- Embody Conscious Awareness.
- Breath is fuel. If it is important enough to say, it is important enough to breathe before I say it.

➤ Sound is expressed emotion.

➤ It is intrinsic to be who we are and essential that we must.

➤ The three Ts—Timing/Talent/Tenacity.

➤ Our mouth is not "our mind out loud." Be strategic!

➤ Our eyes tell the story.

➤ Sovereignty means supreme excellence or an example of it.

➤ Caution creates anxiety; conscientiousness creates awareness.

➤ All tension is fear based.

➤ Everything in life revolves around two things—to choose to do something or not to choose.

➤ The routine is never routine.

➤ Everything in Vocal Awareness is connected to core.

➤ Support means both to support my voice and support myself.

➤ Space has value.

➤ Nothing is gained by going too fast; potentially, everything could be lost.

➤ Surrender means to be in service to the Work.

Principles and Techniques

➤ The Persona Statement—your personal Brand

➤ Mission, Vision, Goals Statements, and Timeline

➤ Stature

➤ The 7 Rituals: The Checklist

1. Thank You to My Source.

2. Love and Let Go.

3. Allow a Slow, Silent, Conscious, Loving Breath.

4. See the Edge and Arc of Sound.

5. Take My Time.

6. Pay Attention/Deeper Listening.

7. Be My Self.

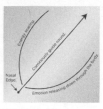

Daily Vocal Awareness Workout

7 Minutes a Day: The Three Aspects

First Aspect

Minute 1: Focus, review the 7 Rituals, center yourself.

Minutes 2 and 3: A combination of the Tongue Pull, Two-Finger, and Pencil Technique Yawn-Sighs.

Second Aspect

Minute 4: The Tongue Pull Yawn-Sigh with text.

Minute 5: The Two-Finger Yawn-Sigh with text.

Minute 6: The Pencil Technique Yawn-Sigh with text.

Third Aspect

Minute 7: Performance.

The Five Pillars of Vocal Awareness

Consciousness

Vision

Integrity

Integration—lead to

Mastery

Visceral Language

Symbol Explanation

1. **CLB = Conscious, Loving Breath**

   This is a slower, deeper, and whenever possible, silent breath. This acronym will remind your unconscious mind to slow down when necessary and will enable you to have more *thinking time* and control. In addition, CLB helps contribute to more vocal strength, expression, and confidence.

2. **/ = A Downbeat**

   This is a musical term. Where you see the downbeat, your unconscious mind will put greater stress—emphasis—on a vowel or syllable. This will, in turn, contribute to your communicating with more authority and enhanced communication dynamics.

3. **✔ = A Catch Breath**

   This is the most fundamental breath we use in everyday conversation, and most often within paragraphs and storylines of prepared speeches. Our habit is we never notice a breath. Particularly in prepared texts, it is imperative to do so in order for the delivery to be as conscious and *natural* as possible. Without this visual reminder, you will forget to breathe in the most appropriate places. Remembering the earlier admonition—*breath is fuel*—you will always run out of gas.

4. **= the 4th Ritual—"To See the Edge and Arc of Sound."**

   This image contributes to maximizing resonance and vocal strength, both critical to performance stamina.

5. (·): *See* the Punctuation

Every time you stop, even if it is not a complete thought, *literally*—not merely figuratively—*see a period*! This could be a difficult concept to grasp, but it is definitely worth the effort.

Each time you see a period, your voice and delivery will convey more definition and strength. Your thought will not trail away—*seeing the period* will enable you to *follow through*. (Remember in Vocal Awareness, we do not speak *to* the end of a thought, we speak *through* the end of a thought.) In addition, the listener/audience's perception is that you are more authoritative and confident.

6. Underlining = Emphasis

Underlining a consonant or a word reminds you to stress that word or sound. This enhances resonance and contributes to more effective articulation, enunciation, and expression. Your message will be clearer and your audience will perceive you as well spoken.

7. T = Transition

This is the connective tissue of storytelling. A transition alerts the unconscious mind of the listener to pay attention. Wherever you place the "T" mentally in spontaneous communication or visually in prepared text, the next phrase will be conveyed with different emphasis. Where the "T" is placed, you may choose to speed up or slow down, be louder or softer, and so on. It is employed when you want to make a definitive point or create a transition to a new thought.

8. W = What?

This is a technique I created many years ago for broadcasters. I have always explained it by saying—"the W/the what" represents a question. Where there is a question, there must be an answer. It helps us listen better.

168 Hour Exercise—Remember, the most important commodity in life is time. When it is gone, you never get it again.

APPENDIX II

Stratagems and Guidelines for Communication Mastery

I encourage you to utilize the following Vocal Awareness principles and axioms to support you on the journey to Communication Mastery. They will provide insight and inspiration and will support you in the integrity of your intention to be the leader you are capable of being.

1. My commitment to excellence includes conscious integration, discipline, and a steadfast step-by-step approach that leads to true accomplishment.

2. I strive every day to be more aware and make valiant choices in order to fulfill my destiny.

3. When I hold my breath, I reflect tension, caution, fear, unconsciousness. When I breathe consciously, I claim myself.

4. Caution creates anxiety; conscientiousness creates awareness. I commit to being conscientious, thoughtful, and aware.

5. Vocal Awareness/Communication Mastery is a commitment to life-altering possibilities that exist when I own my Voice.

6. With Vocal Awareness/Communication Mastery, I have a pragmatic and spiritual foundation upon which I can build a life of honor and success on *my* terms.

7. When I Surrender/Serve/Soar, I create the opportunity to serve my highest ideals and fulfill my possibility.

8. When I communicate from my core—the Hub of my Voice—the same person shows up everywhere.

9. I need not strive for perfection, but rather excellence in everything I do.

10. To be my best, I must practice conscientiously and implement my practice in every professional encounter.

11. To be in Mastery requires Conscious Awareness combined with mind/body/spirit integration.

12. As athletes study their performances, I will do the same— critically but not judgmentally.

13. Freedom without direction is chaos. As I provide direction, I have the opportunity for creating life on my terms.

14. Integrative Leadership requires a commitment to live nobly with clarity of purpose.

15. Everything in life revolves around two things: to choose to do something or to choose not to do it.

16. Even when I abdicate, I make a choice—does that choice empower me or disempower me?

17. To the best of my ability, I commit to making informed conscious and conscientious choices.

18. The meeting begins before I walk in the room. Engage Conscious Awareness; embody Stature.

19. Vocal Awareness teaches self-reliance and Self-awareness. When I embody Communication Mastery, I am an effective communicator.

20. I commit to living in the *sovereignty* of who I am—supreme excellence or an example of it.

21. I am in charge of the *messenger* and the *message*. I only want my audience to know what I want them to know.

22. Eye contact provides a tangible connection with my audience. It enhances storytelling and mental focus and amplifies the sound of my voice.

23. No white noise—no fidgeting, ums/uhs, tapping my toes, drumming my fingers, and so on—these behaviors do not reflect the best of who I am.

24. Integrative Leadership requires vision, trust, dedication, risk—unceasing commitment to excellence.

25. To fulfill my vision, I must establish attainable goals and steadfastly accomplish them in incremental steps.

26. Fundamental to my business plan—I must write down my Mission, Goals, and Timeline and consistently evaluate and update.

27. Character is a choice. I choose to fulfill my promise. Character reflects who I am.

28. Integrative Leadership requires a *strategic action plan* and the passion to make it a reality.

29. In all business dealings, I will strive to ennoble myself and others.

30. Extraordinary success requires Integrative Leadership—intrapersonally and interpersonally.

APPENDIX III

Communication Mastery and Integrative Leadership: Strategic Insights and Tips

A traditional compositional technique for composing a symphony is called ABA—shorthand for statement, development, recapitulation—as you "compose your life book" now is the time to restate essential principles integral to your practice of Communication Mastery and Integrative Leadership.

1. Remember: Everything you do and say must be integrative and reflected in your Persona Statement—your Brand. Each interaction and exchange is an opportunity to connect. This understanding applies to the written word, spoken word, body language, your internal conversation, and so forth. Each element is a part of the whole not an isolated moment.

2. "Don't bury the lead." This is a common term employed in journalism. We can refer to it here as the "headline." Employing this methodology requires that talking points are conveyed through storylines always artfully connected and integrated, not simply conveyed as data, and that they strategically relate to and consistently refer back to your opening line or definitively to the topic at hand.

3. Success is never unilateral. It requires teamwork. To effect success necessitates personal and professional flexibility and adaptability while at the same time maintaining an integral commitment to a stated Vision. Success, in part, is achieved when there is synergy and clarity within yourself and between you and your stakeholders.

4. Visceral Language: Assiduously practice "making voice visual." Annotate your text in Vocal Awareness and practice as outlined in Chapter 5. Pay attention to language, punctuation, and supportive sidebars in the margins of your text. It all matters. Train every day to see your words—this technique alone is a game changer. I tell singing students: "The act of singing is natural, the art of singing is skill." It takes discipline and dedication to sing well. Speaking is natural. To consistently speak commandingly and authentically is an art form.

5. *The only constant in life is change.* Dynamic change requires dynamic action. Dynamic action requires dynamic leadership. Stasis is resistance to change. It is not an option.

6. Always embody the axiom: *It is not only the message but the messenger that matters.*

7. Synergistic consistency through all modes of communication is required—verbal, nonverbal, and written.

8. "Less is more." Choose the language that best embeds your point of view. Deliberately make your point clearly and succinctly. It can take the form of sound bites that compel us to listen and are easily captured by the audience's ear or visually in the way they are written. Sound bites can also be a brief story conveyed through metaphor and/or simile that reveals an action and commensurate outcome.

9. Fear is our strongest emotion—it can propel us to success or vanquish us. The choice is ours.

10. Competition: Never seek to beat anyone else, rather do all that you can to be your best. When we strive to conquer, we impede ourselves.

11. Be proactive, never reactive.

12. Never aspire to competence. To be competent is to acquire a skill or be proficient. Rather, aspire to excellence—a commitment to being distinctive and exceptional.

13. Communication Mastery/Integrative Leadership: Leaders ennoble. They do not subjugate.

14. The theatrical/journalistic axiom: "Who, what, when, where, why" summarizes our strategic tips. *Who* am I? *What* am I here to accomplish? *When* sets goals and timeline. *Where* asks the questions, Where am I going? Where do I want my organization to go? What are my mission and vision and are they compatible with the organization's mission and vision? *Why* is the subtext. It is our subliminal understanding, our internal messaging, that initiates and sustains everything we do.

15. An essential character trait of consummate leadership is humility. Take pride in your work, but be humble. There is a dignity in humility—self-recognition without self-importance.

16. Vocal Awareness is optimistic and trusting. It is optimistic because it believes in possibility. It is trusting because when we do the Work, we create the ability to succeed and fulfill our vision.

17. To fulfill our destiny—transform ourselves and claim our greatness—serving the Work requires a leap of faith.

18. When we practice, we claim. When we claim, we can fulfill our possibility.

19. Mastery requires patience.

20. As you strive for excellence, be forgiving of yourself when you veer off your path or are not diligent in your practice. Simply recognize it, love and let go, refocus and resume.

APPENDIX IV

Leadership Excellence

The following acrostic clearly and concisely integrates the Vocal Awareness Leadership Excellence Principles. Use the acrostic daily to support you in attaining your personal and professional goals.

Leading by example

Empowered/Empowering/Ennobling/Embodying

Anchor/Accountability

Dynamic/Diligent

Excellence/Extraordinary/Ethical

Responsible/Respectful/Reasoned/Reflective

Strength/Steadfast/Safe/Secure/Strategic/Sovereignty

Honorable/Honor

Inspiring/Integrity/Intelligence

Patient/Practiced/Passionate/Purposeful

Standing on Top of the Box

I grew up near downtown Los Angeles, California. In my late teens (17–19 years of age) I would occasionally go downtown to an area called Pershing Square on a Friday or Saturday night, and I would stand on a bench and regale anyone passing by with my uninformed opinions on topics of the day (as though I actually had anything to say)—ah, the ignorance of youth.

A generation later I came up with a leadership program called "Standing on Top of the Box," which refers to the days when public speakers would elevate themselves by standing on wooden crates originally used for shipment of *soap*. These speakers would stand atop soapboxes, to better be seen and heard, the same way I had once stood on a park bench at Pershing Square.

"Standing on Top of the Box" is a leadership program that teaches the difference between being a business leader and embodying a leader in business. I teach this course in corporations, conferences, and at business schools around the globe. "Standing on Top of the Box" is a principle that requires that in business, we do more than simply talk to people and didactically tell them what to do. Rather, it requires a leader to communicate in a way that reflects the discoveries you have made by completing the exercises in Chapters 2 through 4 of this book.

This leadership model, "Standing on Top of the Box," always speaks from two perspectives: intrapersonal leadership (leading ourselves) and interpersonal leadership (leading others). It requires significant accountability as we cannot ask of others what we cannot ask of ourselves. Lastly, it recognizes that we *cannot hold the space for another, but only hold the space for ourselves.* In other words, we can't empower another person, but we can help them empower themselves. The spine of this program is the following Vocal Awareness Leadership Model titled Leadership Excellence.

When I let go of who I am, I become what I might be.

—Lao Tzu

Lead by Example: Leadership is fundamental to each and every one of us as human beings.

I don't want to be intimidated by the concept of leadership—because it is truly accessible. Vocal Awareness is a system, a stratagem, a template that supports me on my journey to revealing the leader I truly *know* myself to be. It begins when I ask myself the questions: How would I like people to know me? What is my brand? How would I like to be perceived? Then I craft a map that is called a Persona Statement in Vocal Awareness. It says, "This is how I want to be known—period." If that persona has value for me, if it's true for me, then I have an ethical responsibility to learn how to *be* that. The notion of leading by example simply says, "Let me be who I am for my Self. Let me embody that which makes me be responsible, respectful, authentic, and learn to claim that consciously—each and every day of my life."

I now have a system that supports me—not just in my meetings or on stage but in the day-to-day living and being who I am. How wonderful!

Empowered/Empowering/Ennobling/Embodying: Empowered to lead. Empowered to ennoble. Empowered to embody.

What is the contribution I am empowered to make? What is the Vision that I hold that ennobles me and others—and how do I manifest it? I *can* choose to live and work from this higher vision. I *can* inspire the people around me and imbue their lives—and mine—with meaning. When I lead by example, from my highest Self, it is not only empowering, it is ennobling. In this process of leadership, I must always speak respectfully. I do not want to speak hierarchically or compartmentally, judgmentally or unconsciously. To be empowered acknowledges that I have something to claim within my Self. It is my right and it requires that I embody it. It is my ethical commitment to me.

My new commitment to Self includes conscious integration, discipline, and a steadfast step-by-step approach that leads to true accomplishment.

Anchor/Accountability: Anchor to my Voice—Voice with a capital "V."

Integrating my inner Voice, my Deeper Self, with my outer voice enables me to claim who I am in synergistic simplicity. To integrate my inner Voice with my outer voice enables me to consistently anchor to the true me. When I am anchored, I am confident, secure, and accountable in being the consummate leader I am capable of being.

Deeper Listening means to listen to my Deeper Self—my inner Voice. When I live in Deeper Listening, I live in the integration of mind/body/spirit.

Dynamic/Diligent: It is so joyful to tap into and integrate my dynamic essence in everything I do.

As a leader, I must be consciously connected to the dynamic energy that flows through me. This energy, this vibration, is at the core of who I am. It is my responsibility to tend to it, nurture it, and develop it to the best of my ability at all times. To live in *conscious connection* to this dynamic energy enables me to live without fear and supports me in living in the energy of Spirit as I dynamically claim my place in the world.

Diligent: from *diligere* meaning "love, take delight in." When I am diligent, I show care and conscientiousness in everything I do. I recognize that caution creates anxiety and that conscientiousness creates awareness. When I am diligent, I am conscientious, aware, and committed to being my best.

There are no guarantees in life. The only thing in my control is how I manage my inner life energetically, vibrationally.

Excellence/Extraordinary/Ethical: Excellence in every moment.

Every moment is a new opportunity to *be* my best. I do not need to concern myself with being perfect because perfection does not allow me to risk, explore, or possibly even make mistakes. All of those things, are part of the nature of learning—a part of my growth process. When I strive for excellence, it supports me in honoring the best of who I am capable of being. To achieve the level of excellence I am capable of requires that I live in mind/body/spirit consciousness. In a word—surrender (to yield or give back). Being in service to all that I represent and all that I believe in accepting—but not merely settling for. I must believe that I can ecstatically live in the excellence of who I am.

Extraordinary: meaning outside the normal course of events. When I commit to being extraordinary, I allow myself to fulfill my Self and never prevent my Self from fulfilling my greatness.

Ethical: To adhere to the principles of right or good conduct. This is my moral compass intrapersonally and interpersonally. My commitment is to integrate this principle not only in what I do but in who I am.

I must never be concerned with being perfect—rather, with living in excellence.

Responsible/Respectful/Reasoned/Reflective: Respectful.

When I am respectful, I am responsible and respectful to my Deeper Self—and my higher Self. I allow my Self the opportunity to fully claim my power in as honest and rigorous a way as possible. When I am respectful and responsible, the leadership decisions I make are more reasoned, reflective, honest, and humble. When I consciously embody respect—Self-respect, respect of Self, and respect of others—I am then in service to all that is possible through my leadership.

When I claim my Self, I have a greater opportunity to be my authentic Self. It helps me be, enjoy, and vigorously embrace who I truly am.

Strength/Steadfast/Safe/Secure/Strategic/Sovereignty: With respect and gratitude, I honor the strategic leader within me.

To serve the Work requires strength of purpose, strength of will, physical strength, and spiritual strength. It takes courage and heart to be the kind of leader I am capable of being. I steadfastly commit to being a safe, secure, and honorable leader—for my Self and others.

As I communicate who I am from the core of who I am, I commit to communicating consciously and steadfastly my best, my deepest, my truest Self to the best of my ability.

Sovereignty: from *souverain* meaning supreme excellence or an example of it. When I embody personal sovereignty, I embrace the right to be who I am. This is one more opportunity to be my Self.

*When I live in Self-acceptance and Self-deserving, I no longer
yearn for the life I envision but actually live it. As I communicate
who I am from the core of who I am, I commit to communicating
consciously and steadfastly my best, my deepest, my truest Self
to the best of my ability.*

Honor/Honorable: Honor my Vision. Honor my Self.

What are my options? I must strive to live an honorable life and,
when I don't, forgive myself and continue the journey. When I
embody the honorable person I am capable of being, life unfolds
effortlessly.

*When I honor my Deeper Self, I live in the synchronicity of the
purity of my deepest intentions—even the unexpressed ones and the
refined essence of my natural vibration. I am the person I deserve to
be and am capable of being.*

Inspiring/Integrity/Intelligence: Integrity and integration have the same root source. They mean "wholeness."

Inspire means to "breathe into." When I live in the consciousness
of my integrated Self, I live in the integrity of who I am—period!
There is nothing else. When I communicate as the inspired leader
I am capable of being, I breathe into others and enable them to
do the same—to be the inspired leaders they are capable of being.
When I slowly *allow breath* (not *take* breath) in this loving, integrated wholeness, I energetically hold the space for others to do
the same. I commit never again to merely motivate—but, rather,
to inspire.

*The root of the word "intimate" is "intimus"—"intrinsic or
essential." It is intrinsic to be who I am and essential that I must.*

Patient/Practiced/Passionate/Purposeful: Passion inspires purpose.

I am passionate when I lead a purposeful life. Passion provides me the stamina to succeed. To achieve this level of steadfast commitment requires patience—and patient practice.

When I live in the inspiring passion of who I am, I consciously embody Source and fervently embody all of who I am.

APPENDIX V

Leadership Terms:
Definitions and Etymology

Understanding the history of language connects our past with our present. It provides specific insight fundamental to the arc of the human condition. Words express who we are and what we feel. Knowledge of word origins—our very roots—dramatically enhances Communication Mastery.

Achieve: To perform successfully. Achieve is related to *chief*. It comes from Old French *achiever* meaning "bring to an end" or literally meaning "bring to a head," which was based on the phrase *a chief* meaning "to a head." The heraldic meaning of *achievement*, "coat of arms," comes from the notion that the escutcheon was granted as a reward for particular achievement.

Allow: To let do or happen, permit. *Allow* comes ultimately from two completely different Latin verbs *allaudare* and *allocare*, which became blended to *alouer*. The first *allaudare* was based on *laudare* meaning "praise," the second *allocare* on *locare* meaning "place."

Anger: A strong feeling of displeasure, or hostility. To make or become angry. The original notion contained in this word was of "distress" or "affliction." English acquired it from Old Norse *angr* meaning "grief," and it is connected with a group of words that contain connotations of "constriction"; German and Dutch *eng* (and Old

English *enge*) mean "narrow," Greek *ankhein* meant "squeeze, strangle" (English gets angina from it) also meant "narrow."

Anxiety: A state or cause of uneasiness or apprehension, worry. Circa 1520 from Latin *anxietaten* meaning "anguish, anxiety, solicitude."

Audacious: Fearlessly daring. From the 1540s meaning, "confident, intrepid." From Middle French *audacieux*, from *audace* meaning "boldness." From Latin *audacia* meaning "daring, boldness, courage," from *audax* meaning "brave, bold, daring."

Authentic: Conforming to fact and, therefore, worthy of trust. Etymologically, something that is authentic is something that has the authority of its *orginal* creator. Greek *authentikos* was a derivative or the noun *authentes* meaning "doer, master," which was formed from *autos* meaning "self" and the base *hentes* meaning "worker, doer."

Awareness; Aware: Having knowledge or cognizance; mindful. English has two distinct *ware* words, but the likelihood is that both come from the same ultimate source—the prehistoric Germanic base *war-*, *wer*. This denoted "watch, be on one's guard, take care," and links with Latin *vereri* meaning "fear" (source of English *revere*).

Behavior; Behave: The manner in which one behaves; deportment. The actions or reactions of persons or things under given circumstances. For much of its history *behave* has been used with reference to a person's bearing and public dignity. The noun *behavior* was formed on analogy with the verb from the earlier *haviour*, a variant of *aver* meaning "possession" from the nominal use of the Old French verb *aveir* meaning "have."

Being; Be: The state or quality of existing, existence. One that exists or has life. One's essential nature. There are four distinct components that make up the modern English verb *be*. The infinitive from *be* comes ultimately from an Indo-European *bheu-*, *bhu-*, which also produced *future* and *physical*. Its Germanic descendent was *bu-*, which signified on the one hand "dwell" and the final element of *neighbor* and on the other hand "grow, become."

Business: The occupation in which one is engaged. Commercial, industrial, or professional dealings. A commercial establishment. Patronage. One's concern or interest. Serious work. An affair or matter. Old English *bisignes* meaning "care, anxiety, occupation." Sense of "work, occupation" from the fourteenth century and modern two-syllable pronunciation from the seventeenth century.

Character: The qualities that distinguish one person from another. A distinguishing feature or attribute. Moral or ethical strength. The ultimate source of *character* is Greek *kharakter*, a derivative of the verb *kharassein* meaning "sharpen, engrave, cut." *Kharakter* meant "engraved mark," and hence was applied metaphorically to the particular impress or stamp that marked one thing as different from another—its "character."

Claim: From the Latin *clamare* meaning "to call out, to cry out." The derivative noun *clamor* is the source of the word *clamor*. The combination of these two sources form the basis of the verbs *acclaim*, *exclaim*, and *proclaim*.

Communication: To make known, impart. The exchange of thoughts, messages. Late fourteenth century from Old French *comunicacion,* from Latin *communicationen*, noun of action *communicare* meaning "to share, divide out. Communicate, impart, inform, join, unite, participate in"—literally "to make common" *communis*.

Compassion: Deep awareness of another. Mid-fourteenth century from Old French *compassion* meaning "sympathy, pity"; from L. Latin *compassionem* meaning "sympathy" and *compati* meaning "to feel pity"—*com-* "together" with *pati* "to suffer."

Compel; Pulse: To force, constrain. "Beat of the blood" comes via Old French *pouls* and from Latin *pulsus* meaning "beating," a noun use of the past participle of *pellere* meaning "drive, beat" (source of English *appeal, compel, dispel, expel, propel,* and *repel*). The derivative *pulsare* gave English *pulsate* and also *push.*

Complex: Consisting of two or more connected parts. Intricate. In the 1650s "a whole comprised of parts."

Complicated; Ply: Containing intricately combined parts. Convoluted. Latin *plicare* meaning "fold," a relative of English *fold* and source of *accomplice, complicate, employ, explicit, imply, pleat, plight* meaning "predicament," and *supplicate.*

Confidence: Trust or faith in a person or thing. A trusting relationship. Self assurance. From Latin *confidens* meaning "self-assurance." To put one's trust or faith in.

Confront: To bring or come face-to-face with, particularly with hostility. To meet, encounter. In the 1560s "to stand in front of" from M. French *confronter* and M. Latin *confrontare* meaning "assign limits, adjoin;" from Latin *com-* meaning "together" with *frontem* meaning "forehead"—sense of "to face in defiance or hostility" is late sixteenth century meaning.

Conscious: Having an awareness of one's environment and one's own existence. Capable of thought, will, perception. From seventeenth century Latin into English *consius* meaning "aware."

Conscious Awareness: A synonym for Vocal Awareness. The word *conscious* is added to *awareness* to emphasize the integration of both internal and external focus required to embody Communication Mastery.

Consciousness; Conscience: A sense of one's personal or collective identity. Special awareness of or sensitivity to a particular issue or situation. Latin *conscire* meant "be mutually aware." It was a compound verb formed from the prefix *com-* meaning "with, together" and *scire* meaning "know" (source of the English *science*). To "know something with oneself" implied, in a neutral sense, "consciousness" but also a moral awareness, a mental differentiation between right and wrong.

Courage: The quality of mind that enables one to face danger with self-possession, confidence, resolution, and bravery. Modern English uses *heart* as a metaphor or "innermost feelings or passions." It was not until the early seventeenth century that it became narrowed down in application to mean "bravery."

Data: Factual information, especially information organized for analysis or used to make decisions. Numerical information suitable for processing by a computer. In the 1640s—plural of Latin *datum* "(thing) given." The meaning "transmittable and storagable computer information" first recorded in 1946.

Discipline: From the Old French/Latin *disciplina* meaning "instruction, knowledge." The Latin word for learner was *discipulus*. It evolved over time to also mean "disciple." These meanings also developed gradually into maintenance of order (necessary for giving instruction).

Do: To perform or execute. To fulfill, complete. To bring about, effect. To render. To put forth. To work at. To work out. (OE) Not surprisingly, *do* is a verb of great antiquity. It goes back to the Indo-European base *dhe*, which signified "place, put."

Ego: *Ego* is Latin for "I" and comes in fact from the same Indo-European base as produced English "I." English originally acquired it in the early nineteenth century as a philosophical term for the "conscious self" and the more familiar modern uses "self-esteem" or more derogatorily "self-importance" and the psychologist's term (taken up by Freud) for the "conscious self" date from the end of the century.

Egoism: The belief that self-interest is the just and proper motive for all human conduct. Egotism, conceit.

Egotism: The tendency to write or speak of oneself excessively and boastfully. An inflated sense of one's own importance, conceit.

Empowerment; Power: To invest particularly with legal power. Authorize. Old Latin *potere* was the precursor of Latin *posse* meaning "be able or powerful" (source of English *posse* and *possible*). Its present participial stem *potent* has given English *potent*.

Energy: The capacity for work or vigorous activity. Exertion of vigor or power. *Energy* comes ultimately from Greek *ergon* meaning "deed," or "work." Addition of the prefix *en-*, meaning "at," produced the adjective *energes* or *energos*, meaning "at work," hence "active" which Aristotle used in his *Rhetoric* as the basis of a noun *energeio*, signifying a metaphor that conjured up an image of something moving or being active.

Esteem: To regard with respect, prize. Originally *esteem* meant much the same as *estimate* does "evaluate, assess." As early as the sixteenth century it had passed into "think highly of."

Ethical: Of or dealing with ethics. Being in accordance with the principles that govern the conduct. The underlying meaning of Greek *ethos* was "personal disposition." It came ultimately from prehistoric Indo-European *swedh-*, a compound formed from the reflexive pronoun *swe-* meaning "oneself" and *dhe-* meaning "put" (from which English gets *do*). Gradually the meaning broadened out to "trait, character" and then "custom." English acquired it, in the sense "distinctive characteristic" (based on the usage of Aristotle) in the nineteenth century. The plural usage of *ethics* meaning "science of morals" dates from the beginning of the seventeenth century.

Excellence; Excellent: The quality or condition of excelling, superiority. Something in which one excels. Of the highest or finest quality, exceptionally good, superb. The underlying notion of *excellent* is of physically "rising above" others. It comes via Old French from the present participle of Latin *excellere*. This was a compound verb formed from the prefix *ex-* meaning "out" and the hypothetical verbal element *cellere*, which evidently meant something like "rise, be high."

Fear: A feeling of agitation or anxiety caused by the presence or imminence of danger. A state marked by this feeling. A reason for dread or apprehension. (OE) "Being frightened" seems to be a comparatively recent development in the semantic history of the word *fear*. In Old English times the verb meant "be afraid," but the noun meant "sudden terrible event," "danger."

Fulfillment; Fulfill: *Fulfill* means "to bring to actuality, effect; to measure up to, to satisfy." *Fulfil* dates from the late Old English period, it originally meant literally "fill full, fill up."

Harmony: Agreement in feeling or opinion, accord. A pleasing combination of elements in the whole. The etymological idea behind *harmony* is "fitting things together"—that is, of combining notes in an aesthetically pleasing manner. It comes via Old French *harmonic* and Latin *harmonia* and Greek *harmonia* "means of joining" hence "agreement, concord," a derivative of *harmos* meaning "joint."

Hubris; Hybris: Overbearing pride. From Greek *hybris* meaning "wanton, violence, insolence, outrage." Originally "presumption toward the gods." Note: *Vocal Awareness has reframed this word, to reflect our intrinsic right to be ourselves without approbation.* It is not arrogant to do so.

Integration: To make whole, unify. From French *integration* and directly from Latin *integrationem* (nom. *Integration*) meaning "renewal, restoration."

Integrity; Entire: Steadfast adherence to a strict moral or ethical code. Soundness. *Entire* and *integrity* have the same source—Latin *integer*. This meant "whole, complete," and was formed from the prefix *in-* meaning "in" and *tag-*, the base which produced Latin *tangere* meaning "touch"; source of English *tactile* and *tangible* (and indeed of *intact*, a parallel formation to *entire* and *integrity*).

Intimate: Originally from the L. Latin *intimus* meaning "inmost." The past participle is *intimare* meaning "to impress, make familiar." Another interpretation of *intimus* is often "intrinsic, essential."

Intuitive: The faculty of knowing as if by instinct without conscious reasoning. A perception based on this faculty. Sharp insight, impression. In the1640s, from Middle French *intuitif*, from M. Latin *intuitivus* from *intuit* meaning "to look at, consider."

Joy: Intense or elated happiness. A source of great pleasure. Latin *gaudere* meant "rejoice" (it came from a prehistoric base *gau-*, which also produced Greek *gethein* "rejoice."

Leader; Leadership: To guide, conduct, escort, direct. To influence, induce. To be ahead or at the head of. To pursue, live. To tend toward a certain goal or result. Command, leadership. An example, precedent. **Lead:** The verb goes back to a prehistoric West and North Germanic *laithjan*. This was derived from *laitho* meaning "way, journey" (from which comes English "load"). So etymologically *lead* means "cause to go along one's way."

Love: Deep affection and warm feelings for another. A strong fondness or enthusiasm. The word goes back to an Indo-European *leuby-*, which also spawned a huge lexical progeny: not just words for *love* (love's Germanic relatives, such as German *liebe* and Dutch *liefde*, as well as the archaic English *lief* meaning "dear" and Latin *libido* meaning "strong desire," source of English *libidinous* but also words for *praise* (German *lob* and Dutch *lof*) and *belief* (German *glauben*, Dutch *gelooven*, English *believe*). The sense *find pleasing* is primary; it subsequently developed to "praise" and, probably via "be satisfied with" to "trust, believe."

Mastery; Master: Possession of consummate skill. The status of master. Full command of a subject. (OE) The Latin word for *master*, *chief* was *magister* (which generally assumed to have been based on the root of Latin *magis* meaning "more" and *magnus* meaning "big," source of English *magnify*, and *magnitude*.

Paradigm; Teach; Paradigm Shift: A radical change in underlying beliefs or theory. (OE) To *teach* someone is etymologically to "show" them something.

Passion: A powerful emotion such as love or anger. Boundless enthusiasm. The suffering of Jesus after the Last Supper. Latin *pati* meant "suffer" (it is the source of the English *patient*). From its past participial stem *pass-* was coined, in post-classical times, the noun *passio*, denoting specifically the "suffering of Christ on the cross."

Pause: To cease or suspend an action temporarily. A temporary cessation. A hesitation. *Mus.* A sign indicating that a note or rest is to be held. Reason for hesitation. Early fifteenth century M. French *pause* from Latin *pausa* meaning "a halt, stop, cessation" from Greek *pausis* meaning "stopping, ceasing."

Perfect: Lacking nothing essential. Being without defect or blemish. Completely suited for a particular purpose, ideal. Accurate, exact. Something that is *perfect* is etymologically "completely made." The word comes via Old French *parfit* from Latin *perfectus*, the past participle of *perficere* meaning "finish."

Performance; Perform: To begin and carry through to completion, do. To carry out, fulfill. To give a public performance. If the word *perform* had carried on as it started out, it would now be *perfurnish*—for it comes ultimately from Old French *parfounir*, a compound verb formed from the intensive prefix *par-* and *fournir* meaning "accomplish."

Persona: A voice or character representing the speaker or narrator in a literary work. One's public image or personality. Latin *persona* originally denoted a "mask," particularly one worn by an actor—it may have been borrowed from Etruscan *phersu* meaning "mask."

Possibility; Possible: Capable of happening, existing, or being true. Capable of occurring or being done. Latin *posse* meaning "be able" (source of English *posse*) produced the derived adjective *possibilis* meaning "that can be done."

Potential; Potent: Capable of being but not yet in existence. Latin *posse* (source of English *posse* and *possible*) meaning "be able or powerful."

Presentation; Present: To introduce, formally. To bring before the public. The Latin adjective *praesens* meaning "at hand, now here," originated as the present participle of *pracesse* meaning "be before one," a compound verb formed from the prefix *prae-* meaning "in front" and *esse* meaning "be."

Reality: The world or the state of things as they actually exist, as opposed to an idealistic or notational idea of them. **Real** and its various derivations (reality, realism, realize) go back ultimately to the Latin *res* meaning "thing," a word of uncertain origin related to Sanskrit *ras* meaning "riches." The broader meaning of the word was probably instigated by the reintroduction of the word from the Latin in the mid-sixteenth century.

Respect: To have regard for, esteem. *Respect* and *respite* are ultimately the same word. Both go back to *respectus*, the past participle of Latin *respicere* meaning "look back at," hence, "look at, regard, consider."

Ritual: The prescribed form of a ceremony. A system of ceremonies or rites. *Ritual* was borrowed from Latin *ritualis*, a derivative of *ritus* meaning "religious or other ceremony or practice" (from which, via Old French *rite*, English gets *rite*.) It may have been related to Sanskrit *riti-* meaning "going, way, custom."

Self: One's total being. Individuality. One's own interest or advantage. From Germanic related to *selbe*. Where it came from is unknown but seems to be related to various pronouns denoting "oneself."

Self-esteem: To respect and honor my uniqueness—my Self.

Soar: To rise, glide, fly high in the air. To climb swiftly or powerfully. Late fourteenth century from Old French *essorer* meaning "fly up, soar" from V.L. *exaurare* meaning "rise in the air," from Latin *ex-* meaning "out" and *aura* meaning "breeze, air."

Solitude: The state of being alone. A secluded place.

Soul: The animating and vital principle in humans often conceived as a immaterial entity that survives death. Related to the Greek *aiolos* meaning "quick-moving."

Source: A point of origin. A *source* is etymologically something that has "surged" up. The word comes from Old French *sourse* meaning "spring," a noun use of the feminine past participle of *sourdre* meaning "rise, spring." This in turn was derived from Latin *surgere* meaning "rise," source of English *surge*. The notion of the "place where a watercourse springs from the ground" led on naturally to the metaphorical "place of origin."

Sovereignty: Supremacy of authority or rule. Supreme excellence or an example of it. From mid-fourteenth century, "preeminence," from Anglo-Fr. *sovereynete*, from O.Fr. *souverainete*, from *soverain*, meaning "authority, rule." From *sovereign*—someone who is "above" others.

Space: A period or interval of time. A little while. *Space* comes from Old French *espace* from Latin *spatium* meaning "distance, space, period." A word of unknown origin.

Spirit: The animating force within human beings or the soul. The part of the human being associated with mind, will, and feelings. Latin *Spiritus* originally meant "breath." It was derived from the verb *spirare* meaning "breathe" (source of English *aspire, conspire, expire, inspire, perspire, respire, transpire*), which probably came ultimately from the prehistoric Indo-European base *spies-* or *peis-*, imitative of the sound of blowing or breathing out. But, in the Augustan period, it gradually began to take over as the word for "soul" from *anima* (source of English *animal* or *animate*) which itself originally denoted "breath."

Stature: The natural height of a human or animal in an upright position. The meaning circa 1300 "height" from Old French *stature*, from Latin *statura* meaning "height, size of body, size, growth" from *stare* meaning "to stand" from PIE root *sta-* meaning "to stand."

Strategic/Strategy: A plan of action. The art or skill of using stratagems as in policies and business. Etymologically, *strategy* denotes "leading an army." It comes ultimately from Greek *strategos* meaning "commander-in-chief, general" a compound noun forms from *stratos* meaning "army" and *agein* meaning "lead."

Stress: Importance, significance, or emphasis placed on something. A state of extreme difficulty, pressure, or strain. To subject to pressure or strain. *Mus.* Accent or a mark representing it. From 1300— "to subject (someone) to force or compulsion."

Surrender: To relinquish possession or control of another because of demand or compulsion. To yield or give back. To *surrender* is etymologically to "give up." The word was borrowed from Old French *surrender* meaning "deliver over, give up," a compound verb formed from the prefix *sur-* meaning "over" and *rendre* meaning "give, deliver." It does not mean to quit.

Take: To get possession of, seize, or capture. Now defunct relatives include Middle Dutch *taken* meaning "seize" and Gothic *tekan* meaning "touch."

Tension; Tense: The act of stretching or condition of being stretched. A force tending to stretch or elongate something. A strained relationship between people or groups. The adjective *tense* was adapted from *tensus*, the past participle of Latin *tendere* meaning "stretch." It originally meant simply "stretched tight," and the metaphorical "strained" did not emerge until the nineteenth century.

Transformation; Transform: To change markedly in appearance or form. To change in nature or condition. Convert. Mid-fourteenth century from Old French *transformer* from Latin *transformare* meaning "change the shape or form of," from *trans* meaning "across" and *formare* meaning "to form."

Value: A fair equivalent or return for something. Monetary or material worth. Worth as measured in usefulness or importance, merit. A principle, standard, or quality considered worthwhile or desirable. To have *value* etymologically means to be "strong" or "effective" and hence to have "worth." The word was borrowed from Old French *value*, a noun use of the feminine past participle of *valoir* meaning "be strong, be of value."

Virtue: Moral excellence and righteousness, goodness. An example or kind of moral excellence. A particularly efficacious or beneficial quality. Latin *virtus* meaning "bravery, strength, capacity, skill, merit" was derived from *vir* meaning "man;" source of English *virago* meaning "man/woman" and *virile* and so etymologically it denoted "manliness." It passed into English via Old French *vertu*. Derivatives include *virtual*, which preserving another semantic aspect of its source, originally meant "having power, in effect" but by the seventeenth century it had evolved into its modern sense "so in effect or in essence" and *virtuoso*, which was borrowed from the Italian and goes back to the ancestral sense meaning "skill."

Visceral: Of or situated in or affecting the viscera. Intensely emotional. Instinctive. In the 1570s meant "affecting inward feelings" from M. French *visceral* from M. Latin *visceralis* meaning "internal" from Latin *viscera* meaning "internal organs"—of unknown origin. The bowels were considered the seat of emotion.

Vision; Visa: The faculty of sight, eyesight. Unusual foresight. A mental image produced by the imagination. A *visa* is etymologically something that is "seen." The word comes from the French *visa* meaning literally "things seen," a noun use of the neuter plural form of the past participle of *videre* meaning "see" (source of English *vision* and *visit*).

Voice: Sound produced by the vocal organs of a vertebrate and/or human. The ability to produce such sounds. Expression or utterance. A medium or agency of expression. The right or opportunity to express a choice. *Voice* comes via Old French *vois* from Latin *vox* meaning "voice" whose other contributions to English include *vocal*, *vociferous*, and *vowel*. Its ultimate source is the Indo-European base *wek-* meaning "speak, say," which also produced Latin *vocare* meaning "call," ancestor of English *vocation*.

Work: Physical or mental effort or activity. A profession or other means of livelihood. A duty or task. "Work" is at the center of a small family of English words that go back ultimately to Indo-European *werg-, worg-* meaning "do, work."

Sources:

The American Heritage Dictionary, 4th ed. (Boston: Houghton Mifflin Harcourt, 2006).

John Ayto, *Arcade Dictionary of Word Origins: The Histories of More than 8,000 English-Language Words* (New York: Arcade Publishing, 1993).

Online Etymology Dictionary, http://etymonline.com.

APPENDIX VI

Quotations to Live By

The following is a series of wise thoughts, practical notions, inspiring ideas that span centuries. We all have our own. Here are a few of mine. They are words to live by. I encourage you to employ The Three Aspects and practice speaking them aloud. Practice annotating them in Visceral Language.

The only person you are destined to become is the person you decide to be.

—Ralph Waldo Emerson

Success does not consist in never making mistakes but in never making the same one a second time.

—George Bernard Shaw

All men make mistakes, but only wise men learn from their mistakes.

—Winston Churchill

I believe that we learn by practice. Whether it means to learn to dance by practicing dancing, or to learn to live by practicing living, the principles are the same. In each, it is the performance of a dedicated precise set of acts, physical or intellectual, from which comes shapes of achievement, a sense of one's being, a satisfaction of spirit. One becomes, in some area, an athlete of God. Practice means to perform, over and over again in the face of all obstacles some act of vision, of faith, of desire. Practice is a means of inviting the perfection desired.

—Martha Graham

Everyone has his own specific vocation or mission in life; everyone must carry out a concrete assignment that demands fulfillment. Therein he cannot be replaced, nor can his life be repeated, thus, everyone's task is unique as his specific opportunity to implement it.

—Viktor E. Frankl

For millennia women have dedicated themselves almost exclusively to the task of nurturing, protecting, and caring for the young and the old, striving for the conditions of peace that favor life as a whole . . . The education and empowerment of women throughout the world cannot fail to result in a more caring, tolerant, just, and peaceful life for all.

—Aung San Suu Kyi

Solitude gives birth to the original in us, to beauty unfamiliar and perilous—to poetry.

—Thomas Mann

The years, of which I have spoken to you, when I pursued the inner images, were the most important time of my life. Everything else is to be derived from this.

—Carl Jung

A mind that is stretched to a new idea never returns to its original dimension.

—Oliver Wendell Holmes

*Those who dance are considered insane by those who
can't hear the music.*

—Anonymous

*Between stimulus and response there is a space. In that space is our
power to choose our response. In our response lies our growth
and our freedom.*

—Viktor E. Frankl

Honesty is the best policy.

—Miguel de Cervantes

Not all who wander are lost.

—J. R. R. Tolkien

*Some men see things the way they are, and say why, I dream of
things that never were, and say why not.*

—Robert F. Kennedy

*We are what we repeatedly do. Excellence, then, is not an act,
but a habit.*

—Aristotle

ENDNOTES

Introduction

1. "Judgment," *The Concise Oxford American Dictionary* (New York: Oxford University Press, 2006), 482.

Chapter 1

1. Anthony Everett, *Cicero: The Life and Times of Rome's Greatest Politician* (New York: Random House, Inc., 2001), 29.

Chapter 2

1. Henry Miller, *The Tropic of Capricorn*, www.henry-miller.com.
2. John Ayto, *Dictionary of Word Origins,* (New York: Arcade Publishing, Inc., 1993), 390.
3. "Voice," *The American Heritage Dictionary*, 4th ed. (Boston: Houghton Mifflin Harcourt, 2000), 911.

Chapter 3

1. "Spiritual" and "Pragmatism," *Webster's Twentieth Century Dictionary of the English Language*, unabridged (New York: Publisher's Guild, 1941).
2. Mark Logue and Peter Conradi, *The King's Speech* (London: Quercus Press, 2011), 61.
3. Ibid., 61.
4. Ibid., 67.
5. Ibid., 70.
6. Ibid., 99.
7. Ibid., 125.
8. Ibid., 128.
9. Ibid., 137.
10. Ibid., 137.

Chapter 5

1. Karen Dietz, PhD, conversation with Arthur Samuel Joseph, November 5, 2012.
2. Ibid.
3. Steve Jobs, Special Event, iPod launch, October 23, 2001.
4. Malcolm Gladwell, *Outliers: The Story of Success*, (New York: Little, Brown, & Co., 2008).
5. Seth S. Horowitz, "The Science and Art of Listening," *New York Times*, November 11, 2012.

Chapter 7

1. Martin M. Chemers, *An Integrative Theory of Leadership* (Mahway, NJ: Laurence Earlbaum Publishers, 1997).
2. Ibid.
3. Los Angeles Philharmonic Association website, 2013, www.laphil.com/philpedia/ludwig-van-beethoven.

INDEX

ABOUT THE AUTHOR

Arthur Samuel Joseph, MA, founder and chairman of the Vocal Awareness Institute, has studied the physiological, psychological, and spiritual aspects of the human voice for over five decades. His trademarked and proprietary method, Vocal Awareness™, is designed to provide highly specific techniques to enhance vocal presence, range, usage, depth, command, storytelling, body language, expression, and stamina.

Joseph's varied client list includes business leaders, world-class athletes, broadcasters, actors, singers, and politicians. A sought after keynote speaker and educator, he was a professor at the University of Southern California's School of Theatre, a visiting artist at both Yale and George Washington Universities, and a teacher of graduate extension programs at New York University. Voted Best of the Best by the Young Presidents' Organization (YPO), a global network of young chief executives, Joseph teaches Communication Mastery at corporations throughout the world and has developed a series of workshops, books, CDs, DVDs, and online seminars.

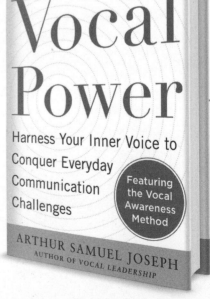